CYLINDER MUSICAL BOX DESIGN AND REPAIR

H.A.V. BULLEID

ALMAR PRESS
4105 Marietta Drive
Binghamton, New York 13903

Library of Congress Cataloging-in-Publication Data

Bulleid, H. A. V. (Henry Anthony Vaughan)
  Cylinder musical box design and repair.

  Bibliography: p.
  Includes index.
  1. Music box. I. Title.
ML1066.B84   1987   789'.8   87-1779
ISBN 0-930256-16-6

First Edition, First Printing . . . June 1987   R 00652 28354

Printed in the United States of America

Cover Designed by James Weaver Graphic Design
Typesetting by Eastern Graphics

CONTENTS

PREFACE

Open the back cover of a fine watch! If you are a novice you might gaze in wonder and ask the question, is all this necessary just to keep time? If you are an amateur or hobbyist you might appreciate the fact that this mechanism could be made at all. As a technician or horologist, maybe you will look at it with full understanding of who and what brought it about and also appreciate its excellent precision and ability to keep time to a fraction of a second.

So, it is with this book. It has appeal for the novice, who may read it just because it is interesting and entertaining. The amateur or hobbyist will find new and factual material to be added to his knowledge. The technician or professional repairman will find his thinking is challenged in a most rewarding way.

All who aproach the book either through casual reading or careful study will come away having learned more about the wonderful world of Musical Boxes.

H.A.V. Bulleid is knowledgeable about all phases of the musical box. He has that English wit and sense of humor which gives his writing a marvelous conversational style. A considerable amount of the book consists of the Authors' writings in the "The Music Box", The Journal of the Musical Box Society of Great Britain. Mr. Bulleid has reorganized these articles, added much new material and provided all of us with an excellent new reference book on all phases of the musical box.

James R. Feller
Past President, Musical Box Society International.
Currently, Trustee and Librarian.

INTRODUCTION AND ACKNOWLEDGMENTS

This book consists mainly of articles published in the magazines of the UK and USA Musical Box Societies, whose members first suggested that they would be useful in book form and then added that comprehensive indexing and extra illustrations would be desirable. I have taken their advice.

In these articles I naturally avoided duplicating the excellent basic data and advice given, for example, in the Graham Webb and Ord-Hume books. My aim was to delve deeper into practical details and their underlying theory.

The larger ("cartel") cylinder musical boxes differ from other antiques and artifacts in that there are virtually no two alike. For this reason explanations of many individual boxes are necessary to give even a modest overall picture.

Enjoyment of musical boxes is enhanced when the mechanism and case are in perfect condition, hence Chapters 6 to 8; and further enhanced by knowing the source of the old but still very popular music, hence Chapter 9. There are many truths to be learned by studying fiction, hence Chapter 10.

I acknowledge with many thanks the loads of help I have received from Dr Robert Burnett, Cliff Burnett, Jim Colley, C W Cramp, James R. Feller, Mike Gilbert, Keith Harding, Patrick McCrossan, Arthur Ord-Hume, Olin Tillotson, David Tallis, Grace and Alfred Thompson, and Graham Webb. They all know a great deal about musical boxes and are ready to share. Other helpers include Dr Britton, Professor Doak, Mr S.G. Morrison and the Swiss Tourist Office.

It is a slight joke among those long interested in cylinder musical boxes that if you decide a particular box is unique you will hear about another just like it within a month. This is due to the fact that the total number seen is far too small to constitute a statistically significant sample. Hence the special need for group help, and so thanks again to the above group.

H.A.V.B.
Ifold, Sussex.
November 1986.

1

CYLINDER MUSICAL BOX THEORY

The overwhelming majority of cylinder musical boxes with cylinders longer than about five inches are of the same basic design . . .

The drive is by powerful spring, key or lever wound, with Geneva stop-work to prevent over-winding and to cut out before the spring runs down.

The music programme is on a brass cylinder with steel pins which lift and suddenly release the tuned steel teeth of the comb.

Playing speed is regulated by a governor whose gear train terminates in a worm gear carrying adjustable fan blades which provide an air brake.

For tune change, the cylinder is moved along its arbor one tune at a time by a retractable peg engaging a snail cam. Cylinder pins for the tunes not in play pass between the tips of the comb teeth.

The mechanism is mounted on a brass or cast iron bedplate. This is firmly secured to the sides or bottom of a wooden case which acts as a sound board.

It is a proven design which remained in vogue with scant alteration throughout the cylinder musical box era—about 1825 to 1895.

It is not fool proof. If the governor assembly is upset or loosened while the spring is wound up, the cylinder will rotate out of control at high speed doing grave damage to the pins and to the comb teeth.

Despite this, and other hazards, very large numbers have survived for well over a hundred years and are still, after restoration, as good as new. This speaks well for the detail design and the underlying theory, both examined in this Chapter.

An important detail of cylinder musical box design is that the cylinder pins are moving towards the tips of the comb teeth throughout their contact. This obviates any reciprocating motion of pin on tooth which would increase wear and cause stray noises and damper troubles. It is achieved by placing the tooth tips considerably above the axis of the cylinder as shown in the large-scale drawing herewith, Fig. 1-1.

All cylinder boxes are set up in the same way, with an angle of 15° between the plane of the comb and a line from the tooth tips to the centre of the cylinder. This important angle is usually achieved by setting the comb at an angle of 7° to the bed plate and with the tooth tips about ¼ inch above the axis of a 2 inch diameter cylinder, and rather more for a larger cylinder. The same basic principle is applied in disc boxes.

The intermesh of the cylinder pins with the bass tooth shown in the drawing is 0.025″ giving a lift of about 0.07″. If a shorter treble tooth had the same intermesh it would have the reduced lift shown of about 0.055″, which explains why the bass end tips should be set a good 0.01″ below the treble tips—"about half a dot" is the classic advice. But note also that the lift at the treble end should be restricted to a maximum of about 0.04″, so the treble end of the comb is set to a reduced intermesh of about 0.015″.

The cylinder pins do not "strike" the teeth; they gently lift them—at a speed of about a tenth of an inch per second which equals 30 feet per hour. It would take two hours for a single run at cricket, not fast. What matters in a musical box is a clean, sudden release of the lifted tooth. I have shown a radial and a raked pin in the large scale drawing and it is easy to see that the release is cleaner from the raked pin, as was described by Alfred Thompson on page 28 of *The Music Box* Vol. 6 No. 1. The thinner the pins the less this matters, and it is also debatable whether it makes much practical difference despite the undeniable theoretical advantage of raking, which also reduces the bending moment on the pins as they lift the teeth.

Judging by the innumerable tune sheets proclaiming "Spiral Steel Dampers", (which persisted long after it had become a Blinding Glimpse of the Obvious) the musical box makers must have been very well pleased by this notable improvement; and the spiral shape is technically well described because in a spiral the radius of curvature is proportional to the distance measured along the curve. In a damper the sharp curvature of

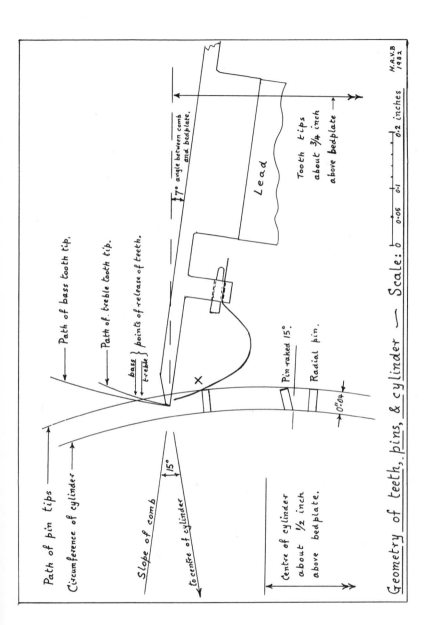

Path of pin tips
Circumference of cylinder
Path of bass tooth tip.
Path of treble tooth tip.
bass
treble } points of release of teeth.

Slope of comb
15°
to centre of cylinder

Centre of cylinder
about ½ inch
above bedplate.

Pin-raked 15°.
Radial pin.
0".04

7° angle between comb
and bedplate.

Lead

Tooth tips
about ¾ inch
above bedplate.

H.A.V.B
1982

Geometry of teeth, pins, & cylinder — Scale: 0 0.05 0.1 0.2 inches

Fig 1-1 Action of cylinder pins on comb tooth and damper.

3

the bottom loop gradually eases till the end near the tooth tip is almost straight—it presents just a slightly convex surface to the cylinder pin which first touches it at the point marked X on the drawing and then pushes it inwards and upwards to touch and then slide along the tooth. Dampers at the bass end need not be quite so close to the tooth tip as at the treble end where the intermesh is less.

It is easy to visualize, from the large-scale drawing, that a damper with less slope is liable to be nipped between pin and tooth, resulting in no damping and a metallic click. Conversely, if the damper end is too curved it will not slide easily along the tooth and may cause premature lifting of the tooth and more unwanted noise. The normal practice of applying a touch of oil to all cylinder pins by means of a card lightly smeared with oil is an important aid to the sliding actions.

It can also be seen from the drawing that even a correctly-shaped damper can be nipped if the comb is too close to the cylinder. This emphasizes the importance of making certain that the comb is completely overhauled and has then been correctly positioned and firmly dowelled, before fitting the dampers.

The damper ends slide easily along the teeth if cleanly cut and I think stoning of the ends is unnecessary. Nor is it necessary to test that every damper will slide along its tooth; but when so testing an occasional damper it is well worth remembering the first point made in these notes, namely that the cylinder pin is moving *towards* the tooth tip throughout its contact with the damper.

Vibrating Teeth

From the earliest days of musical boxes the makers undoubtedly realized the importance of adding richness to their music by achieving the longest possible life of vibrations each time a tooth was played. They found that this depends, for a given lift, mainly on using tempered spring steel for the tooth and having it very firmly anchored. It also depends slightly on the accuracy of the lift, the ambient conditions, and the tooth geometry.

It is therefore reasonable to narrow the problem by saying that in a well set-up musical box all these desiderata are met; and therefore the outstanding question for spring steel experts is "What type of spring steel and what hardening and tempering procedure should be used to achieve maximum life of tooth vibrations?"

4

For some months I have taken this question around Libraries, Research Associations, manufacturing experts and Universities, and I think it is fair to say that nobody knew the answer. The reasons given were that the problem "has no practical application" and that it "is not met in manufacturing industry." Indeed the research people of a well-known engineering consultancy firm said that they always sought the very opposite, trying to minimise vibration. Also the problem is clouded by obscure and complex but very minor factors which might possibly affect the results, such as magneto-electric effects and what were described to me as "the many micro-mechanisms which cause non-elastic behaviour".

However, persistence pays and I eventually exposed this gap in metallurgical knowledge to a Lecturer in Metallurgy at the University of Surrey, Guildford, — Dr. John Britton. He took a kindly interest, sounded the opinions of colleagues, and helped me with the difficult parts of the following notes. . .

The two criteria for sustained vibrations are (1) the application of adequate elastic energy and (2) the tooth material having minimum internal damping.

(1) The applied energy is the force exerted on the tooth multiplied by the distance lifted. This force depends on the modulus of elasticity (Young's modulus) of the tooth steel which should be as high as possible. To allow a good life without any possibility of a permanent set in the tooth a steel with high elastic limit (yield stress) is also needed.

(2) Internal damping is caused by sub-microscopic defects, known as dislocations, in the crystal structure of the metal. These absorb energy by internal friction and, though impossible to eliminate, should be at a minimum.

These two criteria are wholly met in spring steel which has been quenched from red heat and then tempered to about purple colour (275°C) by reheating to that temperature and again quenching. The microstructure of spring steel in this state is extremely uniform, and this same desirable uniformity persists in alloy steels such as silver steel and gauge plate, both of which are commonly and correctly used for replacement teeth. One can see this uniform crystal structure on specimens examined under an electron microscope, and there is no doubt that this uniformity plus the physical properties mentioned above are what give long life to the vibrations.

Going one stage further, after achieving sustained vibrations, what of the resulting musical note? It depends for its tuning or pitch solely on the number of vibrations per second, and for loudness solely on the amplitude of the vibrations. The number of vibrations per second and therefore the pitch depends solely on the geometry of the tooth, though of course the same pitch can be generated by an infinite number of variations of tooth size and shape and tuning weight. It is these variations which add a quality of "tone" to the bare facts of pitch and loudness.

Then why does one sometimes find a comb tooth vibrating for a shorter time than its neighbours? Assuming it is clean and not partly cracked nor with loose damper or weight, the reason must be either a local lack of homogeneity in the steel (not unreasonable in 1850) or a local error in hardening or tempering. Most likely the last; and sometimes the colours of subsequent retempering can be seen on the undersides of a few teeth.

Despite contrary opinions, I am bound to report that there is no evidence whatever that the "tone" is in any way affected by the type of spring steel used for the teeth. Any spring steel of any analysis made to the same dimensions and appropriate temper will sound exactly the same and will differ only, if at all, in the time vibrations take to decay. For most musical boxes the audible range of decay time in the middle range of notes is about five to six seconds. The necessity for rigid anchorage to a mass of metal increases in importance as tooth weight increases towards the bass end.

Quality factors

In a musical box there are four basic quality factors in the music, *volume, aftersound, pitch*, and *tone.* Each of these, in a mechanical instrument with rigidly-mounted steel comb and adequate sound-board, has a completely technical basis, as follows . . .

Volume of the sound emitted by the tooth vibrations is proportional to the work done by the cylinder pin in lifting the tooth. It depends on the amount of lift and the stiffness of the tooth. The stiffness depends on the geometry of the tooth and on the tooth metal.

Aftersound depends on the work done lifting the tooth and on the internal damping of the tooth metal.

Pitch depends solely on the geometry of the tooth.

Tone depends on the tooth geometry and the accuracy of lift and release and on the avoidance of excessive lift which introduces undesirable harmonics.

By the tooth geometry, I mean all its dimensions including where relevant an added tuning weight. It was soon established by the early makers that there was an optimum range of dimensions for good tooth performance, and equally that by small changes in dimensions teeth of the same pitch could be made of different stiffnesses and therefore of different loudness for a given lift.

It is easy to understand how a tooth continues to vibrate until the work done in lifting it is dissipated by internal friction in the metal; but the work can be wasted and the aftersound and tone impaired if the following requirements are not satisfied . . .

1. Comb rigidly attached to its support (eg, no air pockets in the solder between comb and brass or iron base)
2. Comb rigidly screwed to bedplate.
3. Tooth metal free from cracks.
4. No loose parts on tooth (*eg*, loose damper pin)
5. No dirt stuck to tooth.
6. Tooth lifted along its centre-line (if lifted to one side the vibrations may form a figure-of-eight pattern which affects tone)
7. Tooth cleanly released after lift (this needs a sharp and square edge to the tooth tip and preferably release from the edge of a raked cylinder pin rather than from the surface of a radial pin)

Tooth Measurements

It is not possible to give really precise dimensions for the length, width, and thickness of comb teeth, because all three are to some extent indeterminate. So in quoting dimensions, I always stick to the following conventions . . .

Length measured from root to tip, which is significantly shorter than if measured to the end of the slit at the top of the comb.
Width measured at half length.
Thickness measured at thinnest part.

All three are slightly suspect when used in stiffness calculations, and would be unacceptable for absolute values, but the errors all work the same way when comparing the stiffness of teeth and so stiffness ratios are not seriously affected.

7

Emotional Impact

Even when everything is in order, opinions expressed in comparing musical boxes are often emotionally biased by any assortment of these factors . . .

1. The tune playing
2. The arrangement
3. Type (*eg*, bells)
4. Effect of another box just previously heard
5. Placing of the musical box. If placed on a carpet it will not compare with one placed on a table.
6. Surrounding conditions (*eg*, hot, noisy)
7. Frame of mind of the listener (*eg*, after a good dinner) and even, in many circumstances,
8. General appearance of mechanism and case. By about 1850 most makers changed from plain to rosewood-veneered lids with fine marquetry patterns to enhance appreciation of their products.

I expect most listeners would admit to all these. Owners should remember that not many people want to hear all of the tunes a musical box can offer played straight through. Also, serious music lovers may not like some of the abbreviated versions, until they get to appreciate them as being rendered by a unique musical instrument.

Acoustics

Over the years I have heard many comments on musical box acoustics, ranging from the obvious to the bizarre and including so many contradictions that I thought some expert advice would be helpful. Southampton University has an Institute of Sound and Vibration Research which has enjoyed high prestige for many years. Their Professor of Acoustics is Professor P E Doak who, besides knowing all about this extensive subject, is a keen pianist and a good explainer. So I visited him with two typical musical boxes, both with 13 inch cylinders and one with drum and bells, and I report as follows. . . .

To radiate an adequate volume of sound a sounding board is necessary. The classic example is the tuning fork; you set it vibrating but it is almost silent till the stem is pressed on to a surface which it can set into vibration so that strong pulses are sent out into the air. Other typical sounding boards are found in the violin, (whose body receives the string vibrations via the bridge), and in the piano.

The sound one hears from a musical box depends on three factors. . . .

1. The energy applied by the cylinder pins to the comb teeth.
2. The efficiency with which this energy is converted into vibrational energy of the sounding board and, to a lesser extent, of the bedplate.
3. The efficiency with which this vibrational energy is converted into radiated sound.

In a cylinder musical box the base of the case is the sounding board which receives its vibrational energy mainly from the bedplate legs, or from the blocks to which some later movements are screwed.

Sound waves radiated by the sounding board emerge through the clearances cut in the sides and ends of early boxes and all around the feet of later boxes. These sound waves are enhanced by reflection if the box stands on a reflecting surface (a table) as opposed to an absorbing surface (a carpet).

The transmission of the vibrations to the sounding board depends on the comb teeth being intimately clamped to the bedplate, hence the numerous securing screws. The material of the bedplate is not significant so long as it has a high modulus of elasticity such as brass or cast-iron.

Any loose components on the case or the mechanism will start to vibrate whenever a music frequency occurs of the same pitch as its own natural frequency. In doing so, despite the aggravating noise it sometimes kicks up, it only removes a negligible amount of the vibration energy of the system.

Extra components in the case such as drums and bells (when not playing) and tune indicators and tune changers have practically negligible effects on the volume and the performance of the music. The same applies to the non-music comb teeth operating bells, etc. whether they are in a separate comb or integral with a music comb.

If any tooth starts to vibrate in sympathy with another tooth, then obviously it has received its vibrational energy not from a cylinder pin but from the vibrating mass of the comb, which it has thereby diminished—though probably by a negligible amount.

The size of the case considerably affects performance, because the larger the case the greater the radiating efficiency of the bass notes. I think

9

we have all observed this as an advantage of the later, larger cases. In the early years of the cylinder musical box, larger and therefore more effective cases were a natural and fortunate result of the larger diameter cylinders in overture boxes. In exactly the same way a 'cello-sized body is necessary to extend the bass range of a violin.

It does not much matter what wood is used for the box and its sounding board base; the thickness and the firmness are a lot more important than the type of wood. I have seen Nicole and L'Epée boxes with oak bases and with performance indistinguishable from normal. A classic example of an ideal sounding board ideally placed is a vertical disc machine standing against a wall—large sounding board fixed directly to bedplate and with excellent reflection. You could easily hear it above the pub hubbub.

The effect of shutting a musical box lid whilst playing is mainly to reduce some of the treble frequencies which are being radiated by both the sounding board inside the box and, to a lesser extent, directly by the bedplate itself. Some of these treble frequencies may include shrill or unpleasant harmonics, so they are probably better curtailed. There are also those occasional high-frequency clicking sounds which nobody wants to hear. Hence (as per long tradition) it is generally better to play the box with the lid closed.

It is not easy to grasp the fact that the movement alone, without a sounding board, radiates practically no sound from the bass end and but little from the treble end. But this is very easy to prove; simply take a movement from its case and support it on sponge rubber pads on a carpet. Then set it going and listen.

Salient features of the theory behind the above observations are as follows. . . .

The speed of sound in air at normal temperatures is about 1100 feet per second, and the corresponding speeds in cast-iron and in brass are respectively about 14,000 and 9,000 ft per sec. The speeds in various woods range from 11,000 to 16,000 ft per sec.

The connection between the speed of sound (Vft per sec), its frequency or pitch (f cycles per sec) and its wavelength (L feet) is given by the simple formula:

$$V = f \times L$$

So for example the note middle C, of pitch 262 cycles per second, has a wavelength in air of L = 1100/262

$$= 4.2 \text{ feet}$$

The efficiency with which a sounding board radiates sound is given approximately by another formula depending on the periphery of the sounding board (P feet) and the wavelength of the sound being radiated (L feet). . . .

$$\frac{\text{Radiation}}{\text{efficiency}} = \frac{(P/L)^2}{1 + (P/L)^2}$$

This formula is used to determine the lowest frequency a sounding board will effectively radiate; a periphery to wavelength ratio down to one half is acceptable—corresponding to a radiation efficiency of $(1/2)^2/(1 + (1/2)^2)$ $= \frac{1}{4}/(\frac{5}{4}) = 1/5 = 20\%$ efficiency. So from the middle C example given above, if the periphery of the sounding board was exactly 2.1 feet then with a note of wavelength 4.2 feet the radiation efficiency would be just acceptable and the lowest note effectively radiated would be the middle C of pitch 262 cycles per second. Lower notes would be audible, but progressively more faintly. This again emphasizes how the bass notes lose out in volume with a small sounding board.

In the accompanying Table I have worked out some typical examples. Frequencies are doubled if you go up one octave, halved if you go down an octave—so for example the pitch of C one octave below middle C is 131 cycles per second. The table also indicates that some musical boxes have one or more notes lower than their sounding board will effectively radiate. The contribution of the extreme bass notes in smaller boxes is decidedly dubious, as you can demonstrate by shutting the lid and counting how many times a chosen bass note can be heard, and then comparing the actual number of times it was played.

Professor Doak has kindly vetted these notes, and says that they are accurate, although rather oversimplified. For more general information about musical acoustics, an ideal paper-back is *Science and Music* by Sir James Jeans.

Comb Teeth

A generally reliable measure of musical box quality is the number of comb teeth. Yet this number is seldom quoted, perhaps because counting is a chore and the considerable danger of losing count is a further deter-

Table 1. Showing the improved radiation efficiency of bass notes in larger boxes. The low limit of fully effective radiation efficiency is generally taken to be 20%

Type of musical box	Early- 10 inch to 11 inch cylinder	Early- 4 overtures 11 inch cylinder	Typical drum & bells 13 inch cylinder	Late 3-bell 6 inch cylinder	Typical large, late interchangeable 11 inch cylinders	15½ inch coin-slot Polyphon
Sounding board dimensions, inches	15 x 5	17½ x 7½	21½ x 11	16 x 9	30 x 9	19 x 23
Sounding board periphery, inches	40	50	65	50	78	84
Longest wavelength effectively radiated, inches	80	100	130	100	156	168
Lowest frequency effectively radiated, Hz	165	132	102	132	84	79
Lowest musical note effectively radiated	e below middle c	c below middle c	g sharp below middle c	c below middle c	f two octaves below middle c	e two octaves below middle c
Radiation efficiency of C, 2 octaves below middle C (65½Hz, wavelength 201 inches)	4%	6%	10%	6%	13%	15%

rent. Not that it matters to one or two teeth, particularly as the numbers are seldom "neat". The common run-of-the-mill 13 inch Nicole has 97 teeth, notable solely because it is a prime number.

If the comb length is C inches and the number of tunes is T, then the number of comb teeth is approximately 60 times C/T. So for example with the Nicole's 13 inch comb playing eight airs, the number of teeth is $60 \times 13/8 = 97$.

A six-inch comb playing eight airs with three bells will have $60 \times 6/8 - 3 = 42$ music teeth.

A 12 inch comb playing ten airs with eight-striker drum and six bells will have $60 \times 12/10 - 14 = 58$ music teeth.

A nine-inch comb playing eight airs two-per turn is of course like a four-air box and will have $60 \times 9/4 = 135$ teeth.

I hope I haven't annoyed anyone with all these inches. If little c is the comb length in centimetres, the formula becomes: Number of teeth $= 24 \times c/T$.

These formulae assume the track width of each individual tooth is $0.017''$, which is the common standard; and conveniently $60 \times 0.017'' = 1$, near enough. Exceptions are mentioned below and for L'Epée in Chapter 3.

Number of Teeth

It must always have teased the sales sector of the musical box makers to decide the most saleable number of tunes for a given cylinder length and therefore an approximately given price. If they had a yardstick for standard high quality, it may well have been the 13 inch (330mm) cylinder playing eight airs with a 96-tooth comb, give or take a tooth or two on the comb and a line or two on the cylinder.

This poses an important but unanswerable question sometimes raised by newcomers to the musical box field,—"What is the least number of comb teeth for a good quality box?" Angels fear to answer this loaded question, but my answer is "70, or in exceptional circumstances, down to as low as 60."

It is noteworthy that the classic hidden bells and hidden drum and bells boxes and early organ boxes always retained at least 70 music teeth. At that time the general aim for quality boxes seems to have been rather over than under 100 teeth.

As the number of teeth is reduced, so the subtleties available to the tune

13

arranger gradually disappear and rather facile, over-simplified tunes result. There must have been battles fought—tune arrangers wanting more teeth and the boss offering less, to keep down costs. Sometimes the tune arrangers must have won, judging by the Nicole 6-air 11 inch cylinder boxes; as Patrick McCrossan points out, there are two distinct types of these boxes. Some have 106 teeth (track width 0.017″) and some 115 teeth (track width 0.016″). The latter, often mandoline type, are a marked exception to the usual Nicole spacing. Another, similar exception is their 6-air 13 inch cylinder Forte-piano box, and yet another occurs with their 2-per-turn 12 inch cylinder type,—all rightly cherished as high quality boxes. They surely indicate battles won by the tune arrangers.

Playing Time

The purpose of the gearing and governor is to regulate the cylinder (or disc) speed and thus to control playing time as intended by the music arranger. The air brake fitted to the endless of cylinder musical boxes had a good range of adjustment and presumably it was a duty at final inspection to set the blades to give the correct playing speed. This range of adjustment also made the gear ratios less critical than is sometimes supposed, as is demonstrated in the accompanying table which includes four Nicole Freres types and some corresponding types by other makers.

Speed control utlimately depends on the ratio in column 8, namely revolutions of the endless per inch of cylinder circumference. This ratio normally lies between 250 and 300, a range of 20% which was well within the range of adjustment of the air brake and could if necessary be further extended by changing the areas of the fan blades. The only ratios outside this range are from two early overture boxes, both well above 300, and from the 1890s batch-produced interchangeable made by Paillard, Vaucher Fils which had a decidedly larger air brake.

The first pinion, column 3, almost always had 12 teeth; the second pinion, column 5, had 10 teeth; and the wormwheel, column 6, 30 teeth. Again the odd man out is the Paillard, where the whole governor is larger with gear sizes and coarser teeth chosen to make manufacture cheaper.

The gear ratio between wormwheel and worm is simply the number of teeth in the worm-wheel; and the pitch of the worm, which has no significant effect on performance, is chosen to match; the smaller the 30-tooth wormwheel, the finer the matching pitch of the worm.

Suppose, as a first guess, that all cylinders were pinned to play at a peripheral speed of one tenth of an inch per second. On this assumption column 9 shows the playing times for the different diameters of cylinders. The anomalies in these figures are seen at a glance, so I have added column 10, giving the different "ideal playing times". I well recognise that this is largely a matter of opinion, and the times here tabled are the average of several peoples' considered opinions. If you accept them, a clear pattern emerges. . . .

Overture and other "fat cylinder" boxes play at a surface speed of 0.09 inches/second. The normal run of standard boxes play at a surface speed of between 0.11 and 0.12 inches/second.

To the question "why should the late Paillard run so fast, at more than 0.13 inches/second?", my guessed reply is that it was merely a further cheapener, reducing pinning costs by 18% compared with the 0.11 inches/second figure, which adds up significantly when you have to manufacture six cylinders for every box.

The speeds given in column 11 have been rounded to two significant figures for clarity, but they remain accurate to within 3%—which is probably closer than the range of opinions on ideal playing time.

Columns 9 and 10, though headed "playing time", actually refer to a complete revolution of the cylinder. I have found that making allowances for the cylinder's rest period is technically unrewarding. It is only necessary to keep in mind that the proportion of playing time per revolution increases with cylinder diameter. The usual gap is a quarter of an inch, which occupies 4% of the circumference of a 2 inches diameter cylinder and only 2½% on a 3¼ inches cylinder. These again are small compared with opinions on ideal playing time, and even smaller compared with the change in playing times from fully wound to nearly run down, which can approach 20%. It is for this reason that, when displaying a musical box for optimum performance, the winding position of the main spring should be taken into account.

I have also ignored the fact that the effective cylinder diameter is increased by the effective radial length of the pins. This makes another difference of around 4%, but conveniently cancels the effect of ignoring the rest period. Including all these small details involves massive calculations which merely distract attention from the salient features. Stop me if I am being too casual.

The figures in the table certainly point to an *ad hoc* approach to gearing,

Table 2. Typical examples of musical box gearing with playing times and governor speeds. The speed range of a governor depends partly on the size of the fan blades, so larger governors can run more slowly. But, this effect is not enough to explain the wide range of speeds shown in column 12, which is really due to the rather casual approach to gearing by the makers, who were content to rely mainly on fan blade adjustments for speed control.

Maker description & cylinder diameter and length in inches.	GEARING: top line gives No. of teeth in wheels and tpi of worms. lower line, revs per cylinder rev.						Revs of worm per inch of cylinder circumference	Playing time in seconds at cylinder speed 0.1 inch per sec	Ideal playing time in seconds	Ins. per sec. of cylinder for ideal playing time	RPM of worm at ideal playing time
	Great wheel	first pinion	first gear	second pinion	worm-wheel	endless worm					
(1)	(2)	(3)	(4)	(5)	(6)	(7)	(8)	(9)	(10)	(11)	(12)
Nicole 24239 3 overture, cyl 2⅞ x 9⅛	192 1	12 16	64 16	10 102	30 102	23 3072	340	90	100	0.09	1843
Nicole 46561 4 overture cyl 3¼ x 12⅛	192 1	12 16	60 16	10 96	30 96	18 2880	282	102	110	0.09	1571
Nicole 34592 2-per-turn cyl 2⅞ x 19¾	172 1	12 14.3	62 14.3	10 89	30 89	18 2665	295	90	100	0.09	1599
Make unknown 4 overture cyl 3⅛ x 13¾	215 1	12 17.9	66 17.9	10 118	30 118	22 3547	361	98	110	0.09	1935

16

Nicole 45888 8 air cyl 2⅛ x 13¼	160 1	12 13.3	50 13.3	10 66.6	30 66.6	22 2000	300	67	60	0.11	2000
Conchon 7481 8 air cyl 2⅛ x 14	156 1	12 13	50 13	10 65	30 65	18 1950	292	67	55	0.12	2127
Langdorff 6622 6 air cyl 2⅛ x 13⅛	136 1	12 11.3	50 11.3	10 56.7	30 56.7	24 1699	255	67	60	0.11	1699
P. V. F. 12588 6 air cyl 2 x 8¼	130 1	12 10.8	50 10.8	10 54	30 54	23 1620	258	63	50	0.12	1944
P. V. F. 117835 Amobean 6 cyls. cyls 1⅞ x 6½	108 1	10 10.8	44 10.8	12 39.6	28 39.6	18 1109	188	59	45	0.13	1478
Lecoultre 11484 4 overture cyl 3⅛ x 11	220 1	12 18.3	80 18.3	10 146	30 146	22 4380	446	98	120	0.08	2190
Nicole 25226 4 overture cyl 3¾ x 15⅜	240 1	12 20	66 20	10 132	30 132	19 3960	336	118	150	0.08	1584
Bremond 16742 6 air cyl 2⅛ x 13	156 1	12 13	50 13	10 65	30 65	22 1950	292	67	60	0.11	1950

and I have no doubt that a search through several boxes of the same make would show similar differences. An important design feature is that the great wheel must not be appreciably smaller than the cylinder, to prevent the cylinder fouling the fan blades. For example the two Nicole overture boxes in the table both have great wheels the same diameter as their cylinders, yet both have the same number of teeth so there is quite a difference in pitch. Contrarywise, the 2-per-turn Nicole, also with great wheel the same diameter as the cylinder, gives it practically the same pitch as the 4-overture box. They do not seem to have worried, so long as the overall ratio was in line with column 8.

Notes Per Second

The mechanical musical box and the hand-operated piano have this in common—there is virtually no limit to the number of notes per second that they can play. Both can increase their striking rate by repeated massive chords and tremolos for all sorts of special effects and for adding contrast to quieter passages in the music.

Given this shared facility, an interesting question is, what is the average note-per-second rate in typical melodies heard on musical boxes and pianos . . . bearing in mind that the artistic ideal rate is well below the available maximum rate.

Pianists can attain a fantastic striking rate. The tremolo exercise in Hanon's classic work of 1900, *The Virtuoso Pianist in Sixty Exercises*, calls for a maximum rate of 38 notes per second. Most of these notes come in chords of two and six notes; and it seems to be generally agreed that single notes or chords played faster than about sixteen per second lose their effect due to blurring.

Musical boxes lack the piano's ability to hold a sustained note so sometimes a sustained trill is substituted. I have measured several of these on different boxes and found many around sixteen notes per second—for example a long trill on a Nicole overture box consists of 180 notes played in eleven seconds, just over 16 per second. Added to the melody being played at the same time, this totals about 24 notes per second.

Composers add variety by contrasting the numbers of notes per second in the various parts of their music. A typical piano score of *Die Fledermaus* has rates from 11 to 21 notes per second; the flower song from *Faust* 8 to 11; *La Donna Mobile* 6 to 12. I measured a Pianola roll of *Roses of the South* and found a range from 9 to 15 with overall average 12.

18

From these typical examples I think it is fair to say the slowest rates in a tune are not much below two-thirds of the average rate, and the fastest not much above four-thirds. Also I think that in a batch of tune sheet tunes the fastest average rate will be about twice the slowest. These assumptions are relevant because, when examining the number of notes per second played by musical boxes, one is limited on cylinder machines by having to average over all the tunes played. (No one has yet volunteered to count the individual pins per tune, whereas it is a simple matter to tot up the total whilst depthing during repinning).

I expect the tune arrangers had a good idea of the ideal notes-per-second rate; and they must have been dismayed when offered too few. Consider the simple case of a typical 6 inch by 1¾ inch cylinder with about 3000 pins and playing for 50 seconds per tune. The more tunes it plays, the fewer the notes per second and the fewer the number of comb teeth. The result is that, though the average number of pins per tooth per tune remains constant, the musical quality falls off rather sharply as shown in this little listing.

No. of tunes	Average cyl pins per tune	Pins per tune per second	No. of comb teeth	Pins per comb tooth	Pins per comb tooth per tune
4	750	15	90	33	8.3
6	500	10	60	50	8.3
8	375	7½	45	67	8.3
10	300	6	36	83	8.3
12	250	5	30	100	8.3

Four tunes allow some mandolin effect whereas with twelve tunes the number of notes per second is less than half of the desirable range. All the teeth remain hard working throughout the range; more complex boxes such as forte-piano have extra teeth for only occasional use and so the average number of pins per tooth per tune is decidedly lower.

The accompanying Table 3 gives the average number of notes per second and the necessary supporting data for several types of cylinder musical boxes. Excluding specials like the Organocleide and the Nicole Mandolin, they all average between about 11 and 13½ notes per second. Interestingly, the only two over 13 are distinctly on the florid side—the

Table 3. Notes per second played by various types of cylinder musical boxes.

Maker Type Serial No. approximate Date	Cylinder length x diameter inches millimeters	No. of tunes	Seconds per cylinder revolution at correct tempo	Cylinder surface speed, inches/second	Cylinder pins Total quantity		Average per tune	Average per tune per second	No. of comb teeth	Average No. of pins per comb tooth.	Ditto per tune.
Paillard V. F. Harpe Eolienne No. 1617 1875	8¼ x 2 210 x 50	6	50	0.12	Main comb Harpe comb Total	2416 1010 3426	403 168 571	8.1 3.3 11.4	53 24 77	46 42 44	7.7 7.0 7.3
Conchon Harpe Eolienne No. 7220 1875	5⅞ x 1⅝ 150 x 40	4	50	0.10	Main comb Harpe comb Total	1700 800 2500	425 200 625	8.5 4 12.5	51 23 74	33 35 34	8.2 8.7 8.5
Nicole Forte Piano No. 40767 1865	17½ x 2⅛ 445 x 54	8	60	0.11	Forte comb Piano comb Total	4033 1561 5594	504 195 699	8.4 3.2 11.6	87 42 129	46 37 43	5.8 4.6 5.4
Ducommun Girod Forte Piano No. 22386 1850	12¾ x 2⅛ 324 x 54	12 at 2/turn	90	0.07	Forte comb Piano comb Total	5144 2096 7240	429 174 603	9.5 3.9 13.4	89 33 122	58 64 59	4.8 5.3 4.9

	Dim (in)	Dim (mm)										
Sallaz & Oboussier Hidden drum & bells No. 2126 1870	11½ x 2	292 x 50	4	55	0.11	Music Bells Drum	2915 453 843	729 113 211	13.2 2.1 3.8	114 15 12	26 30 70	6.5 7.5 17.5
Bremond Mandolin, 10 bells No. 17614 1885	14 x 2⅛	355 x 54	8	60	0.11	Music Bells	5685 515	711 64	11.8 1.1	91 9	62 57	7.8 7.1
Nicole Mandolin No. 41573 1866	11 x 2	280 x 50	6	55	0.11		6038	1006	18.3	115	52	8.7
Make unknown Organocleide No. 5959 1885	17½ x 2⅝	445 x 67	6	75	0.11		7160	1193	15.9	165	43	7.1
Albert Standard No. 6245 1835	7¼ x 1⅝	184 x 40	4	55	0.09		2404	601	10.9	101	24	6.0
Make unknown Harpe Harmonique Piccolo No. 5941 1885	13 x 2⅛	330 x 54	8	60	0.11	Main comb Treble comb Total	4310 1829 6139	539 229 768	9 3.8 12.8	61 32 93	71 57 66	8.9 7.1 8.3

Ducommun Girod (not typical) and the Sallaz & Oboussier (not a leading maker). The Conchon Harpe Eolienne is rather florid; it has more notes per second than the Paillard and decidedly too many on the harp comb.

I think the Nicole Forte Piano is a model of the ideal note rate for this type. It is a bit surprising that the Alibert, which is typical of top quality "earlies," has the lowest striking rate, but the reason is that it is the only one without embellishments. The comparatively low count for the Bremond Mandolin is due to restrained mandolin effect supported by bells.

The many people who do not like the drum effect will see confirmed the disproportionate number of cylinder pins "wasted". Drum sections of cylinders are almost always heavily pinned, because most tunes sport a number of sustained drum rolls.

Note Rate on Disc Musical Boxes

These machines have no inhibitions as to the notes-per-second they are instructed to play by the disc placed upon them, except at the bass end. So the range of rates involved is quite interesting. I take the ubiquitous 15½ inch disc as the "average" for disc machines, and 64 seconds as its intended playing time. I could get no expert to give a ruling on this time, so I have assumed 67 seconds per revolution. These discs have one hundred peripheral driving holes and at this speed they rotate at 1½ holes per second. Between 4% and 5% of a revolution is lost at tune start, hence 64 seconds per tune. My guess is that this varies from about 58 to 70 seconds from fully wound to run down. (Even faster in Pubs where heavy drinkers leaned on the winding handle.)

Polyphon 1086, the Intermezzo from *Cavalleria Rusticana*, has 690 projections giving, with the above assumptions, a rate of 10.8 notes per second. In contrast Polyphon 10457, *A Summer Idyll* from *Hiawatha* (which does not sound florid or over-decorated) has 1160 projections, giving 18 notes per second. I expect wider extremes exist, but basically the discs occupy the same range as the cylinder machines.

2

SPECIAL TYPES

There are several basic types of cylinder musical boxes and of course innumerable hybrids and oddities, some with very fanciful descriptions.

The standard musical box has one cylinder and one comb covering its musical range, though this comb is sometimes made from two or more separate pieces of steel.

The special types described in this Chapter were gradually evolved by most of the makers with the sole aim of enriching the music.

Another family of special types, not here described, was evolved for nonmusical reasons, including longer playing time (by double springs etc); wider range of tunes (by interchangeable cylinders); continuous play of long tunes (by helicoidal pinning etc). These additions are often ingenious and useful but they have no effect on the resulting "Musique de Genève."

Super Mandoline

Purists claim that a mandoline musical box, if it is to deserve its title, must have groups of at least eight teeth tuned to the same pitch. This claim naturally disappoints owners of those many excellent mandoline boxes in which the groups are limited to five teeth. So?

The group-of-eight has the outstanding technical advantage that it enables one note to be held indefinitely, because by the time the 8th tooth is played the first can be played again. With groups of five the time interval is not long enough except at the treble end.

But the group-of-eight has the corresponding disadvantage that it involves a great number of comb teeth. At least ten notes have to be grouped in eights and several more in fives and sixes. This accounts for a hundred teeth, and with reasonable bass support and treble decoration the comb requires at least 160 teeth. For six tunes this means a 16 inch cylinder.

Top class key-wound Nicole and Lecoultre mandoline boxes, made around 1860, played six airs on a 19 inch cylinder and the comb had 198 teeth. They are doubly impressive when playing well because the mandoline effect also gives the effect of a sustained note, sometimes playing the same note twenty or even more times and thereby holding it for about two seconds and filling a gap in the tune arranger's repertoire.

But one could also buy a wide choice of mandoline boxes, typified by the 6-air Nicole with 11 inch cylinder and 115 comb teeth. These boxes had two groups of six and several groups of five teeth. They applied the mandoline effect more sparingly, but always at key points of the tune, and they jettisoned the long-sustained-note effect. Their cylinders clearly display the characteristic grouping of sets of pins along helical lines. They were a lot cheaper and I suspect some people preferred them to the "super mandoline" type which, if all six tunes are played consecutively, do provide a rather strong mandoline dose.

Presumably after spotting the popularity of these groups-of-five mandoline boxes, some makers moved in with what one can only describe as part-mandoline boxes. These can be recognised from their cylinders, which only exhibit a very few of the characteristic lines of pins. They may have only three or four groups of four or five teeth tuned to the same pitch, cannily chosen to give the effect at key points of some of the tunes. These are the boxes about which newcomers enquire, "Is it mandoline?" the cylinder looking a bit ambiguous. The answer must be, "Part mandoline." Unfortunately, rather a small part.

On the above evidence (to which any extension would be very welcome) I think it is reasonable to apply the term mandoline, or tremolo, to all those groups-of-five boxes, whose tune sheets are always so marked. I think we should apply "Super mandoline" to the groups-of-eight, the real McCoy. They were too good. Why else did they fade away after the 1860s?

Organocleide

Some middle-period musical box makers had the excellent idea of extending the mandoline effect to the bass notes and, incidentally, curtailing the top treble notes so as to produce a deep and rather sonorous musical effect. They named movements of this type Organocleide. Despite a thorough search kindly done for me by the University of Geneva the origin of this word cannot be traced. We all surmise that it came from the Greek orgnon (organ) and kleidos (key) presumably because the Greeks extended both these words into musical meanings, as we do. However, it was out of character for the musical box makers to go so highbrow and I suspect a more likely explanation is that they copied the idea from an early 19th century application, namely the Organo-lyricon. That was the name given to a piano combined with an organ imitating the sounds of several wind instruments.

Strangely, the musical box makers complicated their new word by writing it sometimes with acute accent on the first e, and sometimes with dieresis (trema in French) on the i, both simply denoting that the cle and the ide are separate syllables,—because they had decided, wrongly in the opinion of Greek scholars, that kleidos was a 3-syllable word. Certainly in England these accents are disregarded and the word is pronounced with four syllables, rhyming with *nicely applied.*

The tune sheet of a typical but anonymous six-air Organocleide box is illustrated in Fig 5-25; the cylinder is 17½ by 2⅝ inches (444 by 66mm) with 7160 pins and there are 165 comb teeth. The bass-mandoline effect is best described by comparison with a typical high-quality Lecoultre mandoline box having 199 comb teeth. Thus, a above c (440 Hz) is represented by teeth 38 and 39 on the Lecoultre but by six teeth, 44 to 49, on the Organocleide (teeth counted from bass end). Teeth 46 and 47 on the Lecoultre are the same pitch as teeth 83 to 86 on the Organocleide. And the highest Organocleide tooth No. 165, is the same pitch as No. 105 on the Lecoultre. This item is really the most significant,—the Lecoultre has 90 teeth tuned higher than any on the Organocleide.

Figs 2-1 and 2-2 show the bass end of the Organocleide comb and the corresponding bass end of the cylinder.

Another Organocleide box, No. 38005 by C Lecoultre, has teeth Nos. 46

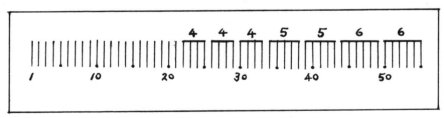

Fig 2-1 Diagram showing groups up to six in the first 55 teeth at the bass end of Organocleide comb with total of 165 teeth. Nos. 44 to 49 are tuned to a (440Hz).

25

Fig 2-2 Bass end of Organocleide cylinder Serial No. 5959 showing typical helical pin groupings for sustained notes or for mandolin effect.

to 48 tuned to a (440 Hz), indicating a generally similar tuning pattern for its comb and confirming the accepted Organocleide range.

Some makers including Bremond and Langdorff sometimes used the alternative and more descriptive title "Mandoline Basse Extra," or "Mandoline Basse Piccolo" (and variations), the latter having the mandoline effect extended into the top treble region.

Mandoline boxes are rightly so called because, though the sustained note effect is achieved, one remains equally aware of the mandoline effect. This effect diminishes with notes of lower pitch, and a much closer approximation to a sustained note results. It was obviously for this reason that the organ analogy first came to mind. Arthur Ord-Hume has appropriately referred to its "basso profundo". Moreover, the sustained note effect is even more pronounced when heard from another room. Keith Harding has encapsulated this feature with a dash of drama during the restoration of Bremond Organocleide No. 10160.—"When I first heard it playing in an upper workshop, I ran upstairs to find what was producing such a wonderful sound!" All I can add to that is, impetuosity rewarded.

Forte Piano

For people with the time and ability to listen carefully there is something peculiarly attractive about a Forte Piano musical box. One hears with pleasure a soft passage repeated *forte*, or topped by powerful chords; and such effects as a soft, distant echo of a passage previously only heard at full power. And of course there are many well-known special applications of the effect such as the famous *piano* passage towards the end of *La Marseillaise*.

With these attributes in mind one cannot help asking three questions: why are Forte Piano boxes comparatively rare, why did everyone stop making them about 1880, and why was the effect never introduced on disc machines???

I think the same two answers apply to all three questions; first, the public came to prefer noisier boxes in the 1880's, and secondly the standard 2-comb Forte Piano arrangement is not cost effective—by definition it involves a large proportion of the comb teeth being inactive for quite long periods. This puts it into the luxury class compared with comb teeth in use throughout, particularly when the trend is towards preferring *forte* to *piano.*

There were many talented workers on early musical boxes and they must have produced many movements with tone and volume variations; but the first chronicled examples of the Forte Piano effect were obtained from a single comb with the cylinder having either long and short pins or slightly and heavily raked pins to give the *forte* and the *piano* respectively by altering the tooth lift. Though there was no problem about using a 2-stage pinning operation to achieve either of these pin arrangements, it seems likely that a great deal of hand work on individual pins was involved, particularly as sometimes there were intermediates between the pin lengths or angles, thereby permitting a crescendo from *piano* to *forte* (and corresponding diminuendo) as on David Lecoultre serial no 9506 which was illustrated with tune sheet on page 178 of *The Music Box* Vol. 9 No. 4. The variations in tooth lift introduced dampering problems, sometimes alleviated by using hooked teeth.

If a single-comb Forte Piano box got damaged and lost its tune sheet it was more than likely to lose its real identity when re-pinned, which I think partly explains why such boxes are so very rare today. But also, probably due to the excessive demands on skilled labour in pin setting and to dampering problems, they were superseded around 1845 by what became the standard type, with about two thirds of the cylinder playing a *forte* comb and one third playing a *piano* comb, and with equal pins throughout the cylinder. The *forte* comb had teeth similar to the general run of combs, while the piano comb had much finer teeth as shown in the Table 4.

The stiffness of a tooth is proportional to the cube of the thickness multiplied by the width and divided by the length. This stiffness in turn is roughly proportional to the work done in lifting the tooth tip a certain distance which determines the amplitude of the resulting vibrations and thereby the volume. For box 40767 the ratio is 195/57, about 3½ to 1, which is more than enough to give a loud/soft contrast but is of course subject to control in setting up the combs.

By the time these 2-comb Forte Piano movements became standard the tune arrangers already had considerable knowledge of the effect, and I think it is fair to categorize their style under three headings. . . .

1. Completely separate *forte* and *piano* passages, varying from short (one or two bars) to quite lengthy.
2. *Piano* passages reinforced with a few notes, generally bass only but sometimes accent or piccolo notes, from the *forte* comb. (Both types one and two often used both combs, mainly towards tune end).
3. Mix of notes from both combs throughout a tune.

Almost any special effect becomes tiresome when flogged and tune arrangers took the natural step towards types two and three for this reason. Most boxes I have heard use type two on some tunes and type three on others, giving a desirable variety without losing the essential Forte Piano charm. The main hazard facing the tune arranger was the fact that the aftersound of a *forte* passage can drown the start of a *piano* passage. This particularly applies to larger boxes and to cases of excessive *forte* volume due to the comb being set too close. This also introduces harsh, undesirable harmonics from excessive tooth lift and the resulting noise is a hopeless prelude for a soft passage of tonal purity. Some late and large Forte Piano boxes, many by unidentified makers, are prone to this trouble though they have many admirers. But it was no use striving for a "powerful" Forte Piano effect; it is essentially subtle and ideally the *forte* is normal full volume and the *piano* a little less than half that volume. The box should stand firmly on a robust and uncluttered table top and be listened to with-

Table 4. Comparison of Forte and Piano Comb Teeth

Maker serial No. & approximate date	Cylinder Length, inches	No. of tunes	Comb type and No. of teeth	Position of α teeth (440 Hz)	Tooth Dimensions in millimeters			Relative stiffness	Stiffness ratio Forte to Piano
					Length	Width	Thickness		
Nicole Freres 40767 1865	17½	8	Forte 87 Piano 42	29 & 30 11 & 12	29.2 26.5	1.98 1.90	0.66 0.43	195 57	3.4 to 1
Langdorff 6622 1852	13	6	Forte 86 Piano 40	28 & 29 9	24.7 21.4	1.83 1.45	0.61 0.53	168 101	1.7 to 1
Langdorff 11258 1858	15¼	4	Forte 162 Piano 55	28 & 29 9	26.0 23.0	1.18 1.06	0.63 0.55	114 76	1.5 to 1
Ducommun Girod 22386 1850	12¾	12 at 2/turn	Forte 89 Piano 33	32, 33, 34 8 & 9	24.6 22.2	1.65 1.78	0.56 0.51	118 106	1.1 to 1
Ami Rivenc 29290 1875	13	4	Forte 115 Piano 70	32 & 33 11 & 12	25.0 20.2	1.24 1.35	0.64 0.48	130 74	1.8 to 1
Unknown maker 11543 1860	13¾	4	Forte 137 Piano 62	45 & 46 13 & 14	25.7 23.0	1.30 1.26	0.66 0.42	145 41	3.5 to 1
Nicole Freres 40200	13	8	"standard" 97	35	26.7	2.24	0.61	190	

Fig 2-3 Nicole Frères 17½-inch cylinder Piano-Forte, Serial No. 40767 Gamme 2261, playing eight operatic airs. The two combs have adjacent treble teeth, a Nicole specialty.

out any extraneous noises, including conversation, if the effect is to be fully enjoyed.

I rather think the arrangers were scared of over-doing the *piano* passage—Nicole No. 40767 has 5594 cylinder pins, of which 1561 are for the piano comb. The combs together have 129 teeth, of which 42 are on the piano comb. So 33% of comb teeth are *piano* but only 28% of pins play them.

Nicole Freres were the makers chiefly associated with Forte Piano boxes and they differed from all other makers in two respects: they called the effect Piano-Forte (in the comparatively rare cases when they so marked the tune sheets) and they arranged the combs with treble teeth adjoining, an elegant refinement because it permits adjacent comb teeth to have equal lift. But it probably caused complications by upsetting the normal routine of the comb makers and of those who set out the pricking programmes. It was probably for these reasons that the other makers kept to the conventional left side for the bass notes.

30

Nicole Piano-Forte boxes are to be found with serial numbers from the early 20,000's (about 1840) right up to the end of their manufacturing business in Geneva in 1880. Popular gamme numbers were often repeated, for example gamme 2261 appeared on No. 40767 mentioned above and on no. 45906 about six years later—it is a collection of eight very popular operatic airs. The same gamme number could be used for both 4-air and 8-air pairs of combs; gamme 1164 appears on straight 8-air and on 2-per-turn 8-air movements. The four most common Nicole types were 17½ inch cylinders playing eight airs, 13¼ inch cylinders playing six airs, and two fat cylinder 2-per-turn types,—eight airs with 9¼ inch cylinder and twelve airs with 13¼ inch cylinder. They all had about 86 *forte* and 42 *piano* teeth, individual boxes varying by one or two teeth and sometimes including unused teeth at the bass end of the *piano* comb.

As usual when writing about cylinder musical boxes of special types, one is hampered by having seen and heard comparatively few—and some of those under very adverse conditions. However, all the Forte Piano boxes I have heard have been of undeniable quality (though some were in urgent need of improved setting) and I have not come across any significant evidence of one maker being better than another. I tend to prefer the smaller ones, among which Moulinié Aîné serial no. 4171, six airs, 13¼ inch cylinder and the Lecoultre mentioned above get my highest mark to date. Langdorff serial No. 6622, six airs, 13 inch cylinder, makes an excellent job of *La Marseillaise*.

Of the larger boxes, some playing lengthy variations on popular tunes or long versions of opera overtures are very desirable; but some Forte Piano overture boxes display the effect with scant regard for the original score which is a natural irritant to music lovers who prefer the loud and soft passages to be as the composer intended.

Forte Piano Specials

Most Forte Piano boxes had about 85 Forte and about 40 Piano teeth; but, in addition to the occasional super-special Grand Format, there were three types of specials: overtures with about 140 plus 60 teeth; mandoline with about 160 plus 60 teeth; and sundries like the Bremond serial no. 29290 mentioned under Ami Rivenc in Chapter 3 which has a 13 inch cylinder playing four airs with 115 Forte and 70 Piano teeth. This is not a mandoline type movement despite the large number of teeth which enable either comb to cover the melody and to add distinctive decoration to the mainly march tunes,—see tune sheet Fig 3-21. The march from *Athalia* is by Mendelssohn, composed in 1845. The most recent tune is from Verdi's *Aida*, 1871.

The comb teeth tuned to *a* (440Hz) are nos. 32 and 33 on the Forte comb and 11 and 12 on the Piano. The stiffness ratio of Forte to Piano teeth is 1.9 to 1, which is in line with the best Forte Piano practice.

Throughout all four tunes there are very few occasions when either comb is completely out of play. With the stiffness ratio a bit less than two to one, there is quite enough volume contrast between the Forte and the Piano, and yet on occasion the Forte is usefully amplified by playing the Piano comb also. Both combs include several sets of three and of four teeth tuned to the same pitch, and though these are not adequate for the mandolin effect they permit notes to be "held" and they also add trills and other decorations to the melody.

Mandolin Forte Piano

The very few mandolin forte piano boxes known are all distinctly different, and there is little doubt that they were regarded as expensive specials. The tune arrangers must have had a lot to say about the comb sizes. Langdorff No. 11258 key-wound with 15¼ inch cylinder playing four airs has 162 forte and 55 piano teeth. Ducommun Girod No. 3787 with 16 inch cylinder also playing four airs has 156 and 76 teeth. Nicole No. 35359 with 21¾ inch cylinder playing eight airs has 122 and 49 teeth.

In comparison, the fairly common and rightly admired Nicole smaller Mandolin boxes playing six tunes with 11 inch cylinders have 115 teeth; Bremond No. 16742 with 13 inch cylinder playing six airs has 124 teeth; large Nicole No. 46516 playing twelve airs with 18½ inch cylinder has 98 teeth; and the early "super mandoline" boxes by Lecoultre and others playing six airs with 19 inch cylinders have about 200 teeth.

So these mandolin forte piano boxes certainly have ample teeth in their forte combs, and the extent of the mandolin effect in the piano sections depends on both the teeth available and the tune arrangements. Only one thing is beyond doubt—more teeth allow more mandolin effect, despite wonders worked by some tune arrangers.

On Langdorff No. 11258 the teeth tuned to *a* (= 440Hz) are Nos 28 and 29 inch the forte comb and no 9 in the piano comb. The stiffness ratio of these teeth is 1.5 to 1, forte to piano. This permits adequate contrast between the two combs while leaving the piano teeth stiff enough to add a bit of volume and a bit of "sublime harmony" effect when, as happens in all four tunes, both combs play for dramatic passages and for the finales.

Most of the 37 teeth at the treble end of the piano comb are tuned in sets of four to the same pitch; and most of the 112 teeth at the treble end of the forte comb are in sets of four and of six, giving a wide mandolin facility. It is an interesting feature of these good mandoline boxes that despite the number of notes played per second there is no feeling of the music becoming florid or over-decorated. The extent of the mandolin effect seems to have been as much a matter of taste as of expense, so perhaps for these special mandolin forte piano boxes wealthy customers may have had a say in the tune arrangements as well as choosing the tunes.

Comparative Loudness

It is generally accepted that for a perceptible increase in loudness the sound energy has to be increased by 25 per cent. This is explained on page 221 of *Science & Music* by James Jeans, Dover Publications, New York. (Library of Congress catalog card No. 68-24652).

About four times this "threshold" difference is needed to give good contrast between loud and soft musical passages, and therefore the theoretical difference required between the stiffness of Forte and Piano comb teeth is not more than two to one. The Langdorff and Ami Rivenc examples in the table come close to this and they give good contrast. Nicole and the overture box of unknown make have decidedly weaker Piano teeth, giving more contrast, but at the risk of the *piano* passages being too soft. However, the human ear is extremely accommodating and all these boxes give very satisfactory performances assuming, of course, that they are listened to in an appropriate setting and without extraneous noises.

The Forte Piano effect is essentially subtle and cannot be emphasized, as some restorers attempt, by setting the Forte comb closer for increased volume. This introduces undesirable harmonics which are annoying to everybody and absolute poison to a musical ear.

Hidden Drum and Bells

When bell boxes were first produced, they must have been called bell boxes, as their tune cards often indicated. Then came the changed fashion of showing the bells and these were often described on their tune cards as "Bells in View". Only with the passage of time did it become necessary to distinguish the earlier type of bell boxes and so the description "hidden bells" (and drum etc) emerged—another typical retroactive description, quite unknown when the product so described was in vogue.

Fig 2-4 Nine bells with bird strikers operated from a separate nine-tooth comb at the treble end of Serial No. 3088, maker unknown.

In a hidden bells box each bell striker is attached directly to its comb tooth, whereas with bells in view the connection is via a link with two pivots and a roller with bearings at each end, and these inevitably allow some lost motion which prevents the same bell being sounded in rapid succession. But a greater factor in the subtlety of many hidden bell boxes is their provision of two strikers per bell, permitting the bell to be struck in as rapid succession as the tune arranger desires.

This same facility was sometimes extended to the hidden drum, some boxes having sixteen drum strikers. This permits a grand sustained drum-roll, with which the arranger sometimes launched one tune on the box, most likely a march. These early bells and drums were far more an integral part of the tunes than in later boxes, which at least partly explains why there was often no provision for disengaging them. When their volume is correctly matched to the music comb and the tunes are well arranged, no one would want to disengage them.

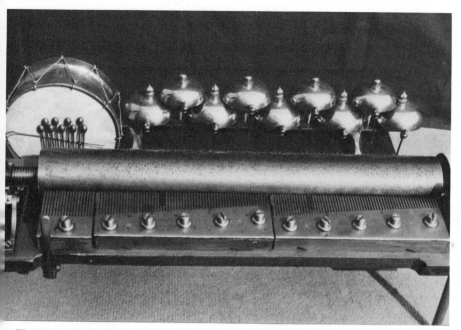

Fig 2-5 Mechanism of drum-and-nine-bells Sublime Harmony Serial No. 12621, 15-inch, 6-air cylinder, maker unknown. It is unusual for having nine drum-strikers and thereby 18 teeth in the separate comb at the bass end. The lever for turning off the bells is missing, for explanation see Fig 2-6. The pairs of teeth darkened are those tuned to *a* (440Hz) indicating the usual Sublime Harmony practice of allowing one comb to cover the extreme bass and the other the extreme treble.

Zither Mania

Zithers on musical boxes are now generally unpopular because neither their muting effect nor their hiding of the comb are liked, and if stored under damp conditions they can accelerate rusting. Yet they had a tremendous vogue starting about 1880, presumably because they cheaply provided an optional variant from normal playing. They were strongly favoured and featured by Paillard, Vaucher Fils; but mainly disdained by Nicole Freres.

The standard application was a ½ inch roll of about eight thicknesses of tissue paper glued into a half-round recess in a wood block mounted un-

35

Fig 2-6 Bell and drum mechanism of Serial No. 12621 seen from below, with the bell On/Off lever removed to show link pivots. Note semi-circular resonator mounted under the drum.

der a fancy metal plate which was usually nickel-plated. It generally covered most of the comb, if not all, and was secured to a bracket held by one of the comb screws. It could be set on or off by a small knob or lever. A minor variant was a screwed knob by which the degree of application could be controlled from just on to fully on.

Occasionally the paper roll of the zither was mounted underneath the comb. In June, 1886, Arthur Paillard patented a device for controlling such zithers by means of a cam on a rod running inside the brass base of the comb, with an operating knob at one end. The patent claimed "When the attachment is applied an observer cannot see what produces the musical effect, which makes the box more interesting".

In another rarely-seen variant the zither was applied only at certain parts of each tune. This was achieved by stepped circular cams, one per

Fig 2-7 Drum, 11 bells and castanet Serial No. 1340 by Ducommun Girod. The eight drum-strikers are worked from the first eight teeth at the bass end of the main comb; the bells and castanet from the separate 19-tooth comb at the treble end.

tune, mounted on the cylinder, which were engaged by a sprung lever attached to the zither.

Undoubtedly the most acceptable zither application is on boxes with more than one comb. Examples are the *Harp, Tremolo* and *Harp, Harmonique* boxes with zithers applicable to one of the two or sometimes three combs; and the *Harp Eolienne* type, having a small second comb with a zither under its teeth, which gives an effective aeolian harp accompaniment to the music from the main comb. Zithers were obtainable as "optional extras" in the 1880s, attached by anchoring under a comb screw. So you can only be certain that a zither was originally fitted if it is fixed directly to the bedplate (as shown in Fig. 2–8) or if it is specified on the tune sheet. Unhappily one sometimes sees the latter type bereft of its zither; perhaps it was simpler to throw it away than to adjust it correctly.

37

Fig 2-8 You can only be quite certain that a musical box always had its zither if it is mentioned on the tune sheet (as zither or harpe) or if it is secured directly to the bedplate as here shown on Serial No. 5255. The On/Off retaining spring with ball end is in front of the central control knob, and the small screws on each side are for adjusting the zither height above the comb teeth.

Automatic Zither

The photograph (Fig. 2–9) shows the mechanism of a considerable rarity among cylinder musical boxes, the automatic zither.

The maker is Paillard, identified only by a simple cross engraved on the governor cock with C/P/&/C in the four corners. The 12 pouces (12.8 inch) cylinder, pinned mandoline style, plays six airs on a 124-tooth comb. The tissue roll in the plain-topped Zither covers all the comb teeth.

At the centre of the cylinder, and displacing only one comb tooth, is a nest of six brass cams which are just greater than the cylinder diameter when the zither is in action, and rise about a quarter of an inch when the zither is to be taken off. The follower for these cams is a finger extending from the centre of the zither. As the cylinder shifts for tune change the fol-

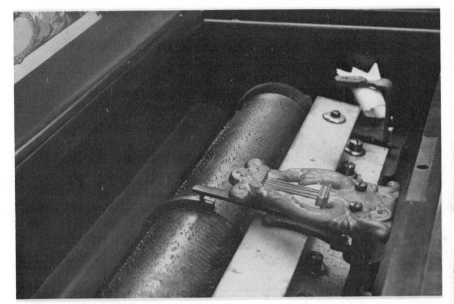

Fig 2-9 Nest of cams on the cylinder, and cam follower attached to the zither, for Paillard's Automatic Zither.

lower comes in line with the appropriate cam. There is no provision for fully disengaging the zither.

I think this idea would have been better applied to a 2-comb box, the automatic zither acting only on the second comb which would act as "harp" accompaniment or decoration to the melody on the main comb. Perhaps just such a box will turn up one day.

Aeolian Harp

An Aeolian harp, so named after Aeolus the legendary God of the Winds, consists of several strings of different diameters stretched over a sound board about three feet long and all tuned to the same fairly low pitch. Eddies caused in wind passing the strings cause them to vibrate and thereby make music; not only does each string sound loudly when its natural frequency matches the varying wind speed, but in addition it sounds some overtones not found in the conventional musical scale. One sometimes heard a similar effect from large arrays of overhead telegraph wires.

Fig 2-10 Typical On/Off lever for Conchon Harpe Eolienne Serial No. 7220, here shown in the On position against the left side stop. The lower end of the lever is a cam, pressing down the spring bar which is pivoted under the bedplate and has lifted the zither to touch the comb teeth. Zither about ½-inch diameter with six coils of tissue paper.

It seems logical to say that if the wind is applied by mechanical means the Aeolian Harp ranks as an item of mechanical music.

Translated into French, it becomes Harpe Éolienne and this attractive title was taken up by Conchon and Paillard and probably others when they were searching for musical box novelties (and sales gimmicks for them) inspired by the idea of applying a tissue-paper zither to the comb. I think the original idea for a Harpe Éolienne box was to have a "harp" accompaniment to the music of the main comb played on a second, smaller comb with a zither under the teeth. Sometimes the zither was fixed, sometimes it was retractable by a sideways-moving lever pivoted to the bedplate in front of the harp comb.

There is no uniformity about the placing of the harp comb; it is at the bass end in Conchon 6822 and at the treble end in Conchon 7220, both

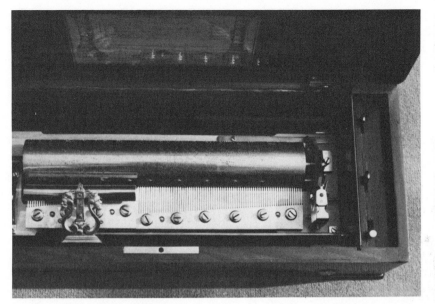

Fig 2-11 Harpe Eolienne Serial No. 43534 of unknown make with harp comb at bass end and zither controlled by a rod in front of the bedplate attached to a third lever on the controls platform.

similar small 4-air boxes. The latter is compared with PVF 1617 in the accompanying table. In both boxes the smaller, harp combs have the more delicate and therefore softer-playing teeth. Paillard's fixed zither obviates the need for any dampers on the harp comb—otherwise about half the teeth require dampers.

The rather casual view taken by the musical box makers of the various "harp" descriptions is illustrated by Conchon 6730, which presumably precedes the two boxes noted above. Its tune sheet is headed Harpe Éolienne and it plays six airs with a 12 inch cylinder and two combs, both covered by a single, conventional on/off zither. I have also seen an unidentified box, again with tune sheet inscribed Harpe Éolienne, having a single 13 inch comb—and, paradoxically, its zither missing.

Of course, no Harpe Éolienne musical box sounds remotely like an Aeolian harp: but with well-arranged and appropriate tunes a quite pleasant,

Table 5. Comparison of Conchon and PVF *Harpe Éolienne* musical box combs, including a comparison of their main comb and harp comb teeth dimensions.

Maker & Serial No.	F. Conchon 7220	Paillard, V.F. 1617
No. of tunes	4	6
Cylinder length x dia., inches	5⅞ x 1⅝	8¼ x 2
Teeth in main comb	51	53
Teeth in harp comb	23	24
Location of harp comb	Treble end	Treble end
Type of zither	Under comb, with On/Off lever	Under comb, fixed
Pitch of lowest harp note	C above middle C 512 Hz	E, two above middle C 645 Hz
Lowest harp note dimensions, thickness/width/length in mm	0.6/1.2/24	0.4/1.3/21
Position of main comb teeth of the same pitch	14th & 15th from bass end	27th & 28th from bass end
Dimensions of these teeth, thickness/width/length in mm	0.8/1.3/22	0.7/1.65/23.5

rather haunting accompaniment to the main music can be achieved. Many listeners have found it agreeable. But the two smaller Conchon boxes mentioned above each have one tune which seems to me unsuitable— 6822 has *Rule Britannia* and 7220 has Mendelssohn's *Wedding March*— both potential thumpers with which you don't mind drums and bells and even a castanette but hardly need plaintive, haunting refrains. The Conchon arrangements are rather florid compared with the PVF, in which the harp effect is more distinctive, despite the fact that the PVF harp teeth are much the weaker, as shown in Table 5.

It would be very interesting to know how far, if at all, the music arrangers were involved in the comparative strengths of the comb teeth; somebody must have prescribed them with care, even where the results were disappointing. A typical successful contemporary Conchon result came with serial No. 7481 playing eight tunes with 14 inch cylinder and tune sheet headed "Harpe Tremolo. Deux Claviers" (two combs). This has a normal type of on/off zither above the tremolo (= mandoline) comb which is at the bass end and has 51 teeth compared with 50 in the main comb. In this box the harp teeth are slightly stiffer and therefore more brilliant than corresponding main comb teeth. This emphasizes a very satisfactory mandoline effect.

Harmonics

When a musical box tooth is lifted and suddenly released, it immediately starts to vibrate at its natural frequency. If for example this frequency is 440Hz (440 cycles per second) it will sound the musical note *a* above middle *c*. However, as with all freely-vibrating members, some parts will have superimposed vibrations of higher frequencies known as harmonics or overtones. These overtones are a small but significant addition to the main frequency and they add a quality factor, *timbre*, to the basic, pure musical note.

The overtones are slightly affected by the way the comb tooth is released. The edge of a raked cylinder pin leaving a sharp-cornered tooth tip gives the necessary instant release, but if this is impaired by wear or misalignment so that the pin scrapes the tooth then further overtones plus undesirable nonmusical noises are likely to be introduced.

More importantly, the overtones are considerably affected by the tooth shape. A tooth required to vibrate at 440Hz can be made to a great variety of combinations of length, width, effective thickness and added weight, and every one will have its own particular pattern of overtones.

Sublime Harmonie

This principle of different overtones in two comb teeth of the same pitch but of different sizes is the basis of the Sublime Harmonie effect. In the normal arrangement the cylinder plays two combs, each with the same number of teeth, (Fig. 2−12). Both combs cover the middle range of notes but the bass end comb carries a few lower bass notes and the treble end comb has a few extra top treble notes. The significant difference between the middle range notes is that those on one comb are dimensionally different from those of the same pitch on the other.

Take for example a typical high-quality Sublime Harmonie movement with 16 inch cylinder playing twelve tunes on two 38-tooth combs, serial No. 15546 made by Baker-Troll, Geneva, in about 1890 when the technique was fully established. All the teeth on the treble end comb are

Fig 2-12 Sublime Harmony Serial No. 39897 made by Ami Rivenc (winged lion on tune sheet) for Dawkins (brass rosettes under comb screws) with 15-inch cylinder and two 54-tooth combs.

longer and wider and slightly thinner than on the bass end. The teeth on the two combs tuned to 440Hz compare as follows. (All measurements in millimetres.)

These comparatively small dimensional differences were found to give the desired effect, and it was important that both teeth of the same pitch should have almost exactly the same stiffness, as achieved in the above example. This ensures that they give the same volume for the same lift, which is important in a Sublime Harmonie arrangement. So the sizes given in this example are quite typical of cylinder musical boxes and of course the same principle applies in disc machines.

Comb	440Hz tooth No. from bass end	Length	Width	Effective thickness	Relative stiffness
Bass	18	26	2.25	0.66	2.49
Treble	9	28	2.84	0.63	2.54

Beats

If two teeth of nearly equal frequencies are sounded together, a periodic rise and fall can be heard in the intensity of the musical note. Because the two notes are very nearly equal in frequency, they keep varying from being exactly in phase to being exactly out of phase with one another, this causing the loud and faint moments respectively. The beat frequency is the difference between the frequencies of the two teeth causing it.

Suppose for example one *a* tooth is tuned to 438Hz and the other to 442Hz, then to the normal 440Hz tone will be added a loud-to-soft beat of frequency 4 cycles per second.

It is generally agreed that this beat effect enhances the Sublime Harmonie effect, but it is difficult to tell how any comb was originally tuned—after the lapse of around a hundred years since it was new. Undoubtedly many were tuned to give this beat effect on the middle-range notes. It was equally possible on any single-comb movement whose comb had at least two teeth of the same pitch, but there is no evidence (as yet) that this was ever done. It is probably due to ageing and damage that one hears beats on some notes in many musical boxes. If you run the edge of a finger-nail along a comb you will often hear beats of various frequencies.

The Patent

The formal launch of what is now always called the Sublime Harmonie effect seems to have come with Charles Paillard's 1874 British Patent No. 3697, simply entitled "Musical Boxes." The significant part reads . . . "The said Invention consists in combining with a revolving cylinder or revolving cylinders two or more separate combs, or two or more series of prongs in one comb plate, and it has for its object to enable me to use shorter prongs, consequently producing vibrations of less duration without that confusion and indistinctness in the melody and in the harmonic accompaniments which are always observed in musical boxes hitherto manufactured and especially those where numerous prongs are used. Each of the aforesaid combs is a complete and independent scale. If I simply wish to obtain a more powerful and harmonious tone than that of other musical boxes, I have only to let the same air be played completely by two or more combs, but if I wish to produce the different shades of musical expression, such as the pianos, the crescendos, the fortes, the decrescendos, I let one or more combs play together, according to the effect I wish to introduce."

"The musical theory of this invention is as follows:—I introduce a very

45

slight dissonance in the tuning of the prongs of the various combs belonging to the same tone, and the said prongs of the same sound being separated, and having a slight dissonance, produce an infinitely more powerful and more harmonious sound than the old style of musical boxes, where prongs of the same tone are placed side by side and tuned at unison, so that the vibrations of the two or more prongs sounding together have a tendency to destroy one another instead of augmenting in volume as is the case with my new system."

"This invention must not be confounded with musical boxes known under the name of "forte-piano," which have two combs, one large and one small. In these boxes the prongs of the latter comb are weakened very much in order to play the soft parts, but only two shades of expression can be introduced, the "fortes" and the "pianos," and in a very different manner from those produced by my invention, where none of the combs are weakened and where the expression is obtained by the use of the same sound in the different combs."

Except for the hint about shorter prongs (as translators then called comb teeth) there is no mention in this famous patent of the overtones effect. Also the two or more combs are definitely stated to be complete and independent scales, whereas all that I have ever seen differ as described above. Nor does the patent lay claim to the description "Sublime Harmonie." But it seems certain that by 1875 everyone agreed both that this patent fathered the Sublime Harmonie effect and that the enhanced tone from such boxes was due to beats effect. This is confirmed in L.G. Jaccard's articles on "Origin and Development of the "Music Box" written in 1938 and reprinted for MBSI in 1967.

To the experts within the industry, however, it must have been obvious very soon that different tooth sizes in the two or more combs were essential to get the desired effect, and the principle was rapidly adopted by several makers. They all inscribed their tune sheets Sublime Harmonie.

Despite this, these boxes are comparatively rare because they were at the luxury end of the market. Their manufacture required separate combs and a greater total number of comb teeth and therefore a longer cylinder than for a comparable single-comb box.

Music Arrangers

It must very soon have become clear to the music arrangers that the Sublime Harmonie effect was only really important in the middle range of notes. It is not needed at the lower bass end and it does not work at the top treble end where the aftersound is very short. So on a typical movement like the Baker-Troll mentioned above the lowest nine notes on the bass end comb and the top nine on the treble end comb would be arranged just as with a single-comb box. But for the middle teeth, the arranger would presumably aim to get the pairs of teeth of the same pitch on the two combs either sounding together or, if the melody made this impracticable, to have them sounding within a second or two of each other, that is while there was still good volume in the aftersound. If you mark one or two pairs of teeth and watch while playing the box slowly, you will see that this ideal was generally achieved.

In the absence of its tune sheet, a 2-comb Sublime Harmonie musical movement can always be distinguished because each comb separately plays most of the main melody throughout, and at the same volume of sound.

I think John M Powell was the first to point out that the real basis of the Sublime Harmonie effect was the pairing of different sized teeth with their different overtones, and this was recorded on page 338 of the Autumn 1982 issue of *The Music Box*, the Journal of the Musical Box Society of Great Britain.

Harpe Harmonique Piccolo

All manner of fancy names were applied to cylinder musical boxes after about 1880, and most of them had no technical or musical significance, being merely the names of various makers' current models.

An exception to this is the Harpe Harmonique, and more particularly the Harpe Harmonique Piccolo which emerged as a recognisable standard type. The date of their first appearance, probably about 1880, is confused by the fact that most of them give no indication of their makers. Some by Baker Troll and Ami Rivenc are known, but most of the others have un-identifiable general-purpose tune sheets and usually also have their serial numbers stamped on the bass end cylinder bearing bracket; this was done by Paillard and Conchon and an unknown number of unknown makers and is no clue to identity.

In addition to the description given as a heading on the tune sheet, all these boxes have two distinctive features: a zither is applied to most teeth of the main comb, which gives the optional "harp" effect when correctly adjusted; and there is a so-called Piccolo comb. This is better described as a

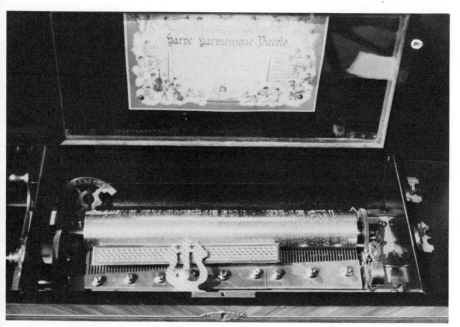

Fig 2-13 Typical Harpe Harmonique Piccolo with 8-air, 13-inch cylinder, Serial No. 5941, maker unknown. Though the zither slightly overlaps the treble comb its tissue is removed at the overlap, and similarly some tissue is removed at the bass end to prevent loss of bass.

treble comb because in practice it seldom carries more than about five teeth tuned to higher pitches than are found on most good single-comb boxes. It is also usual for these Harpe Harmonique movements to have the larger type of case with separate feet and, often, a plinth. Baker Troll made some with interchangeable cylinders and mounted on matching tables. I think it is true to say that all these boxes are lever-wound.

Harpe Harmonique Piccolo movements come with various comb arrangements, but by far the most common type has a 13 inch cylinder playing eight airs. The main comb usually has 61 teeth and the treble comb 32. A typical example is Ami Rivenc serial No. 44136 and they must have been pleased with it because an exact copy of the mechanism and tune sheet (but with different case) appeared with serial No. 44292. Teeth 59 and 60 of the main comb are tuned to the same pitch as tooth 1 of the treble comb, and tooth 61 the same pitch as tooth 2. Exactly the same

2-note overlap is often noted, for example on another unknown maker's serial No. 5044 with 11 inch cylinder and combs of 51 and 26 teeth.

Another box with the 61 plus 32 combs and 13 inch cylinder playing eight airs is No. 5941, again of unknown make. Here the comb teeth overlap further than usual, thus . . .

Main comb teeth	51,52	54,55	56,57,58	59,60	61
Treble comb teeth of the same pitch	1,2,3	4,5	6,7	8,9,10	11

The comb tooth dimensions on these later boxes tend to be rather casual. Teeth on No. 5941 fluctuate in width by up to 0.005″ from tooth to tooth, and in thickness by up to 0.002″. There is also some variation in the position of the thinnest part. Stiffness calculations are therefore rather suspect, but I have done them for all the above mentioned teeth, noting that the treble comb teeth are narrower than those on the main comb, as is usual with these movements. Despite this, all teeth of the same pitch are of approximately the same stiffness—as you would expect. So the only logical motive in placing them on separate combs (with the knowledge available in 1880) would be to achieve the sublime harmony effect. Yet no such attempt was made by the tune arranger for serial No. 5941; the tracks of teeth 51 to 61 on the main comb are very lightly pinned and in fact three of these eleven teeth are almost unused. Also, the occasions of corresponding teeth on the two combs being sounded together are exceedingly few. So the motive of this overlap remains a puzzle, and in any case I think that an overlap as big as eleven teeth on this type of box is rare.

It is also a puzzle why all these boxes have two combs. Perhaps it was a help in production, and especially in getting uniform hardening and tempering. But more likely it was just a sales gimmick—"Superior model, two combs." Some Conchon boxes had their tune sheets inscribed "Deux Claviers." Many single-comb boxes had a good piccolo effect.

The 13 inch cylinder of Harpe Harmonique Piccolo No. 5941 has 6139 pins, of which 4310 play the 61 teeth of the main comb and 1829 play the 32 treble teeth. So the main comb averages 70 pins per tooth and the treble comb 57, which only indicates that the piccolo effect is not overdone.

Another example of the casual attitude to tooth dimensions occurs in Ami Rivenc No. 44292, where for some reason tooth 61 of the main comb and tooth 1 of the treble comb have both been added (undoubtedly by the maker) as separate pieces of steel. Both are wider than their neighbours but of the same stiffness and they are indistinguishable in tone and volume.

It is sometimes stated that the teeth in Piccolo combs are harder than in main combs. I have never seen an example of this, and in all the boxes here mentioned both combs are of the same hardness—that is to say, their teeth have been hardened and tempered in the usual way so that the tips are still comparatively brittle but the tempering has been carried far enough to make the steel malleable for about a quarter of its length from the root. It is quite common to see, in this region, the punch marks made when the teeth were originally corrected for alignment, during manufacture.

All these boxes are decidedly noisier than their predecessors of the 1860s, for three reasons: the comb teeth are slightly stiffer; the sound radiation efficiency is improved by the larger cases having larger soundboards; and the tune arrangers generally employ heavier chords in preference to the quieter and more subtle musical decorations of earlier years. This permitted loud and soft passages, a less subtle form of forte-piano. The style must have proved popular because there were numerous variants on what I have called the standard Harpe Harmonique Piccolo, some illustrating once again the makers' casual attitude to descriptive titles. Tune sheets with inscriptions such as Mandoline Piccolo are found on ordinary Harpe Harmonique Piccolo boxes. Conversely, one finds Harpe Harmonique Zither and Harpe Tremolo tune sheets on boxes which are fundamentally different.

An example of the first is illustrated in Fig. 5–3. It has a 16 inch cylinder playing ten airs with combs of 60 and 32 teeth with the usual 2-note overlap. What is meant by Mandolin Piccolo, one might well ask. There is just one set of four teeth tuned to the same pitch in the treble comb, and never more than three to the same pitch in the main comb. But they are quite cleverly arranged to give many near-mandolin effects.

An example of the second type is illustrated in Fig. 2-14 herewith. This box of unknown make, serial No. 1598, has a 13 inch cylinder playing six tunes. The main comb of 70 teeth at the bass end plays the tunes straight. The second comb with optional zither, has 53 teeth of reduced stiffness. They cover the same range of notes as teeth 16 to 44 of the main comb but with several groups of three and four teeth tuned to the same pitch. It therefore plays a softer, part mandolin version of parts of the tunes. This musical decoration from the second comb is effective both with and with-

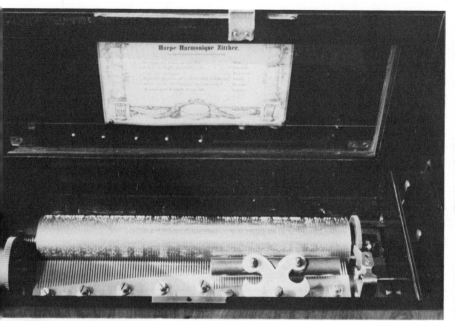

Fig 2-14 This movement uses the treble comb as a mandolin accompaniment, with optional zither effect. As sometimes happens the zither cannot cover the whole comb as it is too close to the governor.

out the zither. It puts the movement into the same general type as the Harpe Eolienne.

A similar arrangement occurs in Conchon No. 7481 with Harpe Tremolo tune sheet, except that the mandolin comb is at the bass end and has teeth rather stiffer than the main comb. This reduces the volume contrast but improves the "harp" effect when the zither is applied to the stiffer comb. The main comb has 50 teeth of which nos 24 to 50 cover the same range as the 51 teeth in the mandolin comb; this limited range permits groups of five teeth giving a more satisfactory mandolin effect.

Organ and Orchestral Boxes

Somewhere around 1870, sets of about seventeen reeds were first added to some musical boxes, their air valves opened by plungers operated from bridges replacing pins on a section of the cylinder. Sometimes pairs of reeds were used, tuned to vary by four to eight cycles per second and so giving a characteristic beat or warble. This rarer type of organ box is correctly described as "Flutes Voix Celestes" (Presumably after the celeste stop of an organ).

Air for the reeds is taken from a bellows below the bedplate pumped by a rod oscillated via a wheel or crank mounted on an extension to the first gear shaft of the governor. The resulting cyclic load, occurring twice per revolution, necessitates a compensated butterfly, preferably with three wings each restrained by light springs so that their braking effect diminishes when the governor loses speed. The considerable extra work demands a stronger main spring. Unfortunately the bellows are rather prone to air leaks which make the organ distressingly "short of puff."

Naturally, some boxes were made with reed organs alone,—rarities and, strictly, not musical boxes. Very nice, though.

The term Orchestral is now applied by general consent only to musical boxes incorporating organ, bells, drum and castanet. It is an adjectival ver-

Fig 2-15 Bremond Orchestral Serial No. 6329, 10-air, 19½-inch cylinder with six bells in view and flute, drum, and castanet. The spring winder is a folding handle on a vertical shaft with pinion driving a crown wheel on the spring arbor.

sion of the original Swiss description *Orchestre* which simply means Orchestra. These boxes were almost always set up with drum at bass end, six or more bells and reed plungers central, and castanet at treble end, —a good display, if rather noisy. But there were exceptions, as in Bremond serial No. 6329 shown in Fig. 2-15. The drum and castanet are hidden below the bedplate, a hangover I think from the early days of drum and bell boxes which gives the advantage of striking hammers fixed directly to the comb teeth. Bremond titled this box "Flutina," see its tune sheet in Fig. 5-9.

Separate levers always permitted the silencing, sometimes mercifully, of drum, bells and castanet; but the option of silencing the organ was rare as it meant retracting the plunger assembly away from the cylinder. Luckily tastes vary; but everyone who really likes the genuine *Musi que de Geneve* should avoid Orchestral boxes which have less than about 65 music comb teeth. Bremond No. 6329 has 72 plus 22 for drum, bells and castanet and 16 levers for reeds, allowing ten airs on its 19½ inch cylinder.

Alternate Tips

There is certainly an interesting mystery about combs with alternate tips.

One finds 13 inch combs of about 124 teeth, all normally tuned to a scale scratched on the brass base, and ready to play six tunes; but only alternate teeth have dampers fitted and the tips of the other teeth have been rather crudely broken off. They are therefore found playing twelve tunes, from a cylinder which usually has a rather densely-pinned appearance.

The end result is threefold. The comb at first sight seems to be fine-toothed; it plays twice as many tunes as expected; and it plays with the quality of a 62-tooth comb, lacking the subtleties expected from an arrangement on 124 teeth.

The question is, why do it? Was the coarse 62-tooth comb thought unattractive? Was the choice of 12 airs in what looked like a conventional 6-air box thought to be a good sales gimmick? For it would seem so much simpler and cheaper to make a 62-tooth comb to suit the job.

A theory put forward is that when a tooth is played, its tipless mate will vibrate in sympathy and produce more sound; but this is technically dubious as explained below, and it certainly was not the intention of the manufacturers, as they took no steps to tune the tipless teeth by adding weight to compensate for the missing tips and damper pins. The result is that the tipless teeth are only in tune with their neighbours at the bass end where their loss of weight is insignificant compared with their total weight. These bass teeth certainly do vibrate when their associated teeth are played, and incidentally can go on vibrating whilst their associated teeth are damped just as can happen with conventional combs; but if they are prevented from vibrating, no change in performance can be detected. I have verified this by making a cardboard "comb" of twenty-five alternate teeth and holding it on the tipless teeth to prevent them vibrating.

An important additional subtlety is that total sound output may even be reduced by unplayed teeth vibrating in sympathy, if their vibrations are out of phase with the playing teeth. This phenomenon was exposed for the more complex case of pianos by an article in *Scientific American* for January 1979. I wrote to the author at the University of Michigan, but his reply merely confirmed the possibility and said that an experimental investigation would be needed to establish and quantify the "alternate tip" possibilities.

Personally, I have no doubt whatever that alternate tips evolved from a production situation in which 12-tune boxes were wanted and there were spare 6-tune combs available. I hold to this view even despite the fact that "big" makers like PVF produced some alternate-tip boxes. I have never seen them on early or late period boxes, which adds some weight to the "force of circumstances" theory. Perhaps a comb-maker mis-read an order and over-produced 6-tune combs—I have never known any production set-up entirely free from such errors. Very occasionally one sees, but would rather forget, a comb similarly adapted but with alternate *teeth*, not just alternate tips.

Let us unite to avoid calling them "alternating tips" as I once saw in an auction catalogue. These tips certainly do *not* go flitting to and fro between neighbouring teeth.

Meanwhile, there are two distinct schools of thought on the intriguing subject. School A holds that with a growing demand for boxes playing more tunes, existing combs in stock had alternate tips removed to permit playing double the number of tunes. School B maintains that the amputation was done purely for quality reasons, on the theory that the tipless teeth, tuned to the same pitch as an adjacent tooth, would vibrate in sympathy with playing teeth and thus add to the overall sound effect. The fact that this theory is a bit shaky, because there is no extra source of energy to create this extra sound, does not put the kybosh on school B which only argues the *motive* for alternate tips, not necessarily the *result*. I suppose there must also be quite a large school C of agnostics, and they may be the wisest.

As a strong adherent of school A, I was distinctly shaken when I first met a 10-air box with alternate tips. Never having seen a 5-air box I made rapid enquiries and found that though very rare there are some in existence; failing that, school A would have had to bite the dust.

Recently I have examined in detail Lecoultre 10-tune alternate tip keywind box serial No. 30490 with 13⅓ inch (335mm) cylinder and 167 comb teeth of which 83 have tips.

The 167-tooth comb has the tuning scale scratched on the brass base, all in groups of 2, 4, or 6 teeth, so that after removing alternate tips every note is still represented. At the bass end all tipless teeth vibrate in sympathy with a neighbour, but fewer and fewer do so as one progresses towards the treble end. Whether any effort to tune them was made is impossible to establish. Nor can one be definite about the sequence or the method of removing the tips; some of the stubs have certainly been ground or filed and it is surprising that they are so variable in length, ranging from completely missing tip to not far short of playing length. And, I wonder why they drilled those 54 damper pin holes for the tipless teeth. I cannot imagine that any of the Lecoultre brothers liked that sort of wasted work and I think it is pretty certain that the comb was made and tuned as a normal 5-air comb. An interesting detail of this comb is that, towards the bass end, where the depth of the brass base is reduced, the tops of the scratched letters of the tuning scale *o la ti ut re me* and *f* are all cut off. *(Sol* was abbreviated to *o* and *fa* to *f)* This proves that they were marked on the brass base before it was adjusted to finished depth.

Tune Selector

Musical Box advertisements in the 1890's and early 1900's sometimes included the following or a similar note . . .

"Attachment for changing tune at will, may be ordered with larger boxes. It is then found between the large Cylinder wheel and lever No. 3, (the change/repeat lever). To obtain any tune on the list, stop the box at the end of the air, then pull the attachment forward the necessary number of times, until the Indicator shows the desired tune."

This type of tune selector normally makes its comparatively rare appearances on late boxes and is nickel plated to match. It works well. The new lever carries a sprung finger which engages a tooth near the top of

Fig 2-16 Tune selector in the tune-change position. The sprung square finger rests on a peg in the bedplate. Each time the lever at the right is pushed back and pulled forward again (at tune end) the snail cam is advanced one tune.

the snail cam and pushes it on one tune. Being sprung it rides over the next tooth on its return stroke. Pegs on the lever bracket prevent excessive movement of the finger, limiting it to exactly one tune when correctly set. The normal tune change/repeat lever is unaffected except that it is pushed to the "repeat" position when the tune selector is operated.

Another and simpler type of "optional extra" tune selector is illustrated in Fig. 2-16. It is on Bremond 8-air, 10-bell box no. 17614 and it entirely replaces the usual tune change lever. The brass bearing block dowelled to the back corner of the bedplate carries a ¼ inch shaft parallel to the cylinder and located axially by two set screws engaging grooves. The treble end of the shaft carries a lever which moves in the slightly widened and lengthened slot of the change/repeat lever. The bass end of the shaft carries a small brass housing for a spring-loaded steel finger with chamfered lower edge and in line with the teeth of the snail cam. When the lever is pulled forward the sprung finger slides freely over the snail cam teeth. When it is pushed backwards the finger swings upwards and advances the cam one tune. A peg is fixed in the bedplate to support the sprung finger in the normal "tune change" position. To leave the movement on "repeat" the lever is pushed right back and the finger is then well clear of the cam. The design is good except for the location of the shaft which should be by fixed collars, the absence of which raises suspicions that it did not originate in Switzerland.

3

THE MAKERS

This Chapter is mostly about what they made, describing many of their products and some of their foibles.

For historical background on the Makers and their involvement with Agents, see Bibliography.

Alibert

It was a characteristic of the Swiss musical box makers that they shared very many design details, due to the many small specialist makers of various components and subassemblies. So, for example, Alibert serial 6245 with 7¼ inch cylinder playing four airs has the same general layout with external controls and the same nonadjustable governor and the same comb screws with dot markings as the Falconnet described below. It only differs substantially in having a comb of standard design with straight tips; and yet it has the earlier type of case with no key partition and with the mechanism let in from underneath and the base secured with a single screw back and front—much less effective as a sound-board than a glued-in base.

Bremond

B A Bremond was a prolific manufacturer of all types of musical boxes and is often claimed to have been the top quality maker of the 1860-1875 period. His cases were above average, some being of exotic shapes and

Fig 3-1 Baker-Troll tune sheet—a type used long after Geo Baker continued on his own. The first tune is more commonly translated as *Tales from the Vienna Woods*.

some including a small automaton at the front. Serial No. 8873 had a colourful drummer beating two kettle drums, seen through a circular window in the case front. Bremond movements are usually identified by their initials stamped on the governor cock. Their tune sheets always had a lyre at top centre, often topped with their distinctive small white cross; sometimes their name was printed on the tune sheet.

A closer look at the Bremond trade mark stamped on the governor cock of serial No. 17614 reveals three errors; it is not central, it leans to the left,

Fig 3-2 The Baker-Troll monogram as seen in gold on leather lifters for glass lids and at lower left on tune sheets; and two arrangements of B A Bremond's initials as seen on governor cocks—sometimes in a circle and sometimes surmounted by a lyre.

Fig 3-3 Another arrangement of Bremond initials carelessly stamped on Serial No. 17614 governor cock.

and traces of the circle and top of the B superimposed on the A indicate a wild previous application. File marks suggest efforts to remove the worst traces of this error.

Such stamps must have been more often applied by apprentices than by craftsmen, which probably explains why they vary in both character and reliability—they are missing on many movements. Probably a new one was only ordered when the one in use was lost or damaged, hence different types, as illustrated.

Makers names stamped on brass bedplates also suffered. Henriot are

60

Fig 3-4 A Conchon trademark, FC and a lyre in separate ovals, sometimes stamped on their governors.

particularly variable and evasive and even Nicole shows occasional signs of a casual apprentice—the upper line NICOLE FRERES is sometimes misplaced and occasionally, as on serial No. 38010, inverted.

Conchon

An interesting letter by Conchon was reproduced on page 186 of *The Music Box*, Vol. 6. It is on Conchon's headed paper, dated 27.11.1891, written in a "clerical" hand, and signed with the rather spiky signature of the boss, F Conchon. The paper twice carries his Star Works trade mark encircling his device of a 5-pointed star threaded through a lyre.

The letter is in French to a customer in London who must have had some special device fitted to a Conchon musical box. The opening paragraph reads . . .

"The mechanism you requested to permit repeating or changing a tune at will has evidently been a complication which we should have refused to undertake, due to its exorbitant cost to me. I hope it will give you the measure of the sacrifices I make, both for my customers and for the reputation of my business."

The letter goes on to explain how to operate "levers Nos 1 and 2 and F and J" and advises the customer, if he still has difficulty, to contact Mr Ch E Brun at 21 Ely Place "who, though the fitting is patented and unknown to him, will certainly be able to explain it to you."

By 1878 Conchon had about 50 employees at his works in Geneva and was making most musical box components himself and supplying some to other makers. He is credited with the first HELICOIDAL box, pinned helically for continuous playing, and he showed it at the 1878 Paris Exhibition. But Conchon boxes are probably best known for multi-comb types, including Sublime Harmony, Harpe Eolienne and Harpe Tremolo, one or more of the combs usually having a Zither.

Conchon only started manufacture around 1874 and his early boxes carry Agents' tune sheets. He was an early user of nickel plating, applying it first to the winding and control levers. By about 1880 he had introduced a number of manufacturing simplifications and economies, compared with his earlier boxes, including fewer comb screws, spaced more widely; coarser machining of bedplate; identical bearing brackets for both ends of the cylinder; iron control levers with plated screwed knobs; and mechanism secured to wooden platforms in the case with three countersunk screws.

These later boxes carried his own tune sheets with the Conchon Star Works trade mark. Some have the lyre-and-star device stamped on the governor block, others have the twin-oval device stamped on the governor cock. Both are illustrated on page 240 of Vol. 8. Between the two ovals are three dots that also feature in Conchon's signature, arranged like the abbreviation for "because".

Judging by Conchon musical box serial number 9594, which was perhaps made around 1882 as its tunes include the Barcarolle from Offenbach's *Tales of Hoffman*, 1881, production had been streamlined by supplying coded finished components to the assemblers; how else can one account for the serial No. 9594 being stamped on both cylinder bearings, both spring brackets, spring barrel and cover, winding lever, great wheel and zither components. Alongside the stamped CONCHON on the brass comb base I regret to report that it appears as 9593, which only goes to show that errors occur even in the best regulated production outfits.

Serial No. 9594 is also stencilled on the iron bedplate (under the gold paint) and on the underside of the case. Only an assembly number, 55, appears on the governor and cylinder and other components. The nickel plating includes the cylinder and the zither assembly.

Conchon No. 7481 was made in 1877 or later, its tunes include the polka from *Les Cloches de Corneville*. (Feb. 1877). It was sold by agents Scotcher of Birmingham who printed their own pattern of tune sheet for it, boldly marked "No. 215". This bogus serial number is of no interest to anyone except perhaps devotees of the agents.

All three Conchon boxes noted in Chapter 2 as Harpe Eolienne have a common feature in their cases which is also unusual: the fronts of the cases are veneered with the grain of the veneer running vertically, in two matching halves.

Most Conchon boxes have their comb or combs stamped CONCH or CONCHON on the brass base which powerfully suggests that either they were not made by Conchon or they left his works at some stage during manufacture or tuning. Otherwise, why label them?

Despite adding rather fancy terms like "Concerto" and "Symphonie" to his tune sheets Conchon seems to have maintained high quality until he closed down in 1898. Perhaps in some respects Conchon was for the 1880s what Henriot was for the 1840s. As E Clerihew Bentley might have put it,

They all say Henriot
Put up a good musical show
But I have a *penchant*
For Conchon.

Ducommun Girod

This highly respected Geneva firm, operating from about 1828 until 1868, was involved in various combinations of partners which may possibly explain why their serial numbers defy reason. The numbers are known from 1000 to at least 30,000 and several 4-figure numbers have been noted on lever-wind movements. However, No. 22386 is a key-wind model

Fig 3-5 Tune sheet of Ducommun Girod, Serial No. 22386, an unusual type. The twelve tunes include waltzes and galops and airs from two Auber and three Donizetti operas, the latest being *Don Pascale*, 1843.

about 1850 or slightly earlier, in plain case with side-hook lid fastening, flap over control levers, and no glass lid. The serial number is written on the bottom of the case with " – /7/50" added which may mean July 1850. The latest operatic tune on the tune sheet, reproduced herewith, is from Donizetti's *Don Pascale*, first performed in Paris, 1843.

Various manufacturing details are shown in Figs. 3-5 to 3-8.

Occasionally one comes across a musical box with so many unusual features that it might be some sort of experiment or prototype or pilot model, as modern manufacturing jargon would describe it. I think Ducommun Girod 22386 comes into this category. It plays 12 airs 2-per-turn with a 12¾ inch by 2 inch diameter cylinder and it has these three distinctly unusual features. . . .

1. Slow-running cylinder taking 90 seconds per revolution and thereby giving nearly 45 seconds per tune.
2. Piano and forte comb teeth of equal stiffness.

Fig 3-6 Mechanism of Serial No. 22386 showing comparatively short piano comb.

3. Piano comb having only just over a quarter of the total number of comb teeth.

Slow Running

The overall gear ratio from cylinder to endless is 1 to 2040, obtained from 136 teeth in the great wheel and conventional 12-tooth and 10-tooth pinions in the governor but the first gear enlarged to 60 teeth. For the cylinder to take 90 seconds per revolution, which is necessary to play the tunes at correct tempo, the endless rotates at 1350 rpm which is at the low end of the practical range and involves the fan blades being at maximum extension. The cylinder surface speed is just under 0.07″ per second. (Details and some comparative speeds are shown in Table 3. This low cylinder speed, which was not uncommon on very early movements, demands greater accuracy in pinning. The playing time is also extended in this case by reducing the gaps between tunes to 5mm—well under a quarter of an inch.

Fig 3-7 Maker's name stamped twice on brass bedplate, once inverted. Quite a rarity.

Fig 3-8 Bass end of Serial No. 22386 cyclinder dismantled for repinning. Small nicks in the edge of the end cap indicate where notches were needed to clear the cylinder pins. Pinning was taken closer than usual to the end of the cylinder.

Tooth Sizes

The teeth tuned to *a* (440Hz) are numbers 32, 33 and 34 on the forte comb   and 8 and 9 on the piano comb. Those on the forte comb are slightly longer, narrower and thicker than those on the piano, but the net result is that they are almost exactly equal in stiffness—the actual ratio, forte to piano, being 1.1 to 1.

To obtain the intended Forte Piano effect the piano comb is so set that the lift of the teeth is reduced.

Comb Sizes

The forte comb has 89 teeth, the piano 33. This compares with the usual split of 82 and 40.

The cylinder has 7240 pins, 5144 forte and 2096 piano. The abnormally large number of pins for the cylinder size naturally follows from the large number of tunes crowded on it and made possible by the low surface speed. Though there are 2½ times as many forte as piano pins the ratio of comb teeth is even greater and in fact the forte comb averages 58 pins per tooth whereas the piano averages 63½.

Performance

As might be expected from the above figures, this movement has distinctly more forte than piano; in fact the piano passages, which are well decorated, are numerous but comparatively brief on most tunes. In addition to the usual bass support from the forte comb, there are occasions when both combs operate together and I think it must have been noted that even at reduced lift the playing of a piano and a forte tooth together added unexpectedly full volume; this is the sublime harmonie effect coming into play. Possibly an arranger or a business rival spotted the effect! It could not be exploited where the music was scheduled for Forte Piano which effect depends mainly on the combs playing separately.

Ducommun Girod serial No. 24042 has the same cylinder size and comb sizes and the same plain case as No. 22386, but it plays its six airs at one-per-turn and it has a weakened Piano comb; so the style of No. 22386 was apparently soon abandoned.

Falconnet

Design and craft details of early musical boxes are doubly interesting by showing the design evolution as well as the style of a particular maker —which is helpful if no other means of identification is available. Some are illustrated herewith, Figs. 3-9 to 3-13.

Falconnet of Geneva was an early maker. One of his lines about 1830 was a 3-air overture type box with cylinder 6¾ inch by 2½ inch diameter and 138-tooth comb. The gear ratio from great wheel to governor worm was 1 to 2790 so the worm made 355 revolutions-per-inch of cylinder circumference (cf 340 in 3-overture Nicole). Playing time at normal musical tempo was about 1 minute 40 seconds, unexpectedly long for a 2½ inch cylinder, giving a cylinder peripheral speed of rather less than 0.08″ per second (cf 0.09″ for the Nicole).

The cylinder pins were radial, not raked, but the comb teeth were hooked.

The comb was made from steel plate ¼ inch thick, about three times the normal thickness, so the resulting thicker pads on the bass teeth meant

Fig 3-9 FALCONNET stamped on thick steel comb; the comb screws with coding dots giving their positions.

Fig 3-10 Falconnet comb showing the thick steel and the separate brass base.

Fig 3-11 Falconnet governor with the early design of fixed lower bearing for the worm shaft.

Fig 3-12 Falconnet three-tune, six-tooth tune-change snail cam.

that fewer teeth needed lead weights. The brass comb base was not soldered to the comb. The comb screws were coded with dots on their heads —no dot on the bass end screw, one dot on the next.

The lower bearing for the governor worm was a brass bracket dowelled to the side of the governor base block, and not adjustable. So, provision of the normal adjustable bearing may have been the last of the major design improvements.

The tune change cam had six teeth, the snail having two sets of three steps so each half turn covered the three tunes. I have seen such boxes wrongly described as having six tunes. The tune change cam follower had a radial screw readily accessible for fine adjustment.

Fig 3-13 Falconnet snail cam follower with an easily accessible screw for fine adjustment.

The movement was housed in a close-fitting plain wood case 12 by 6 by 4½ inches, the three control levers protruding from the left side and the lid having a simple latch, all typical of the period.

The cylinder pinning extended almost to the extreme edges of the cylinder barrel, and all the pins in the tracks of the first bass and the last treble tooth had holes drilled into the end caps to clear them—they were too far in to permit the more usual vee-notches. These holes were drilled right through so that the cement could enter them and seal the pins. The end caps were not pegged to the barrel.

In repinning such cylinders, the pins in the end tracks should if possible be withdrawn after local heating and before pushing off the end caps, whose removal they naturally resist. Of course there is the further hazard in such close fitting that if the treble end cap is not positioned correctly before pinning starts, a lot of extra work is needed to correct it. Falconnet did not attempt that correction on one of his cylinders, and the out-of-line markings recall a craft error of 150 years ago . . . soon forgotten under the influence of the mellow comb and the excellent tune arrangements.

Henriot

One has to face the fact that the early Swiss musical box manufacturers helped each other out and were not fussy or consistent about unimportant details. Not for them the later uniformity of batch production, nor the plugging of their name; they seem to have had no objection to the individual differences of their craftsmen, and their main concern was the quality of the music. These factors add to the charm of early boxes but militate against proving who made which.

Take Henriot for example. Data appeared on pages 169, 254, and 300 of Volume 9 of *The Music Box*, but examination of more boxes shows that some of the clues are not certainties but only probabilities. The bedplate, for instance: most commonly the serial number is stamped along the left side at right angles to the name HENRIOT which is parallel to the cylinder and in the back left corner, as shown on page 169, vol 9. But some practically identical boxes, with compatible serial numbers, lack the name HENRIOT, and others, including twelve-tune 2-per-turn No. 14670, have amplified it by adding a second line "A GENEVE". Most Henriot boxes have brass comb washers. Most have three comb dowels. Some have flat ends behind the tips of the bass teeth. Yet the only single one of all these characteristics that seems to occur on every Henriot box is the serial number running up the left side—and I feel sure someone will soon find an exception to this! But the main point is that a reasonable number of these characteristics taken together will indicate that the box is likely to be by Henriot.

Tune-cards

Another clue is the music, for it has long been held, and so far without contradiction, that Henriot's tune arrangers were top of the league.

Perhaps the most valuable clues lie in the tune cards. Luckily they show a number of characteristics peculiar to Henriot. I list those characteristics which I think occur on every Henriot tune card:

Embossed borders in various patterns.
Tunes not numbered.
Serial number written in central space, not in border.
No. of airs written as heading or up left side, not in border.
Underlining has thickened centre.
Card sizes include 3⅜ by 2¼ inches and 4½ by 3 inches

Fig 3-14 An example of a false clue—here is a transfer label by Nicole Frères claiming to be manufacturers (French; fabricants) applied under the case of Serial No. 15473 which was made by Geo Baker.

72

Only by continually updating our clues as more information comes to light can we refine our knowledge about these admirable early makers of top quality musical boxes.

Langdorff

Thanks to an excellent new discovery by Patrick McCrossan, backed up by information from other Society members, it is established beyond doubt that Langdorff cylinders made before about 1870 have the Gamme number and the last two digits of the year of manufacture scratched clearly on the bass end cap. During this period, from about 1840, their tune sheets had at top centre a square piano; and from about 1850 an upright piano, see Fig. 3-15.

All these early movements had the "Langdorff characteristics" namely. . . .

1. A third dowel pin at the back centre of the main comb (only visible under the comb)
2. Face of comb finished lengthwise

Fig 3-15 Tune sheet of Langdorff Serial No. 6882, made in 1852. The drum (with On/Off lever) and bells being hidden it was logical to mention them, quite modestly, below the list of tunes. In contrast, later bells in view were often proclaimed in heavy lettering.

73

3. Serial number stamped in comparatively large numerals, 4mm or 4½mm high.
4. Brass comb washers
5. Gamme number and last two figures of the year scratched on bass end cylinder cap.

Naturally it is possible that item (2) has been obliterated by a crazy polisher, and the thin brass washers may have been lost and wrongly replaced. The serial number is at the back, base end, of the brass bedplate. Usually it appears alone, but sometimes LANGDORFF is added and sometimes another name—and sometimes with A GENÈVE added.

With all these characteristics in mind it becomes possible to identify more of the "anonymous" boxes of the key-wind and early lever wind period.

These "Langdorff characteristics" also gradually led Patrick to a more far-reaching discovery, namely that some boxes attributed to other makers had all these characteristics *and that their Gamme numbers and year dates and serial numbers fitted exactly into the Langdorff numbering sequence*—as set out in Table 6.

Attribution to Malignon or Moulinié Ainé is sometimes stamped on the bedplate and sometimes inscribed on the tune sheet. Langdorff and Metert were partners from about 1844 until September 1852. All boxes in the table are key-wind except serial 13645.

It has become increasingly well established during the years of existence of the Musical Box Societies that several names associated with cylinder musical boxes were not makers but merely agents or associates. Well known examples are Thibouville-Lamy, A and S Woog, Dawkins, and Nicole for serial Nos. above 50,000. One has to be very cautious about adding to the list, but I think there is now little doubt that Moulinié Ainé can be added. The clues that this renowned watch maker did *not* manufacture musical boxes are . . .

1. He never exhibited musical boxes
2. No distinctive Moulinié Ainé tune sheet is known
3. Despite high serial numbers noted, the boxes are astonishingly rare.

Conversely, the clues that Langdorff made these boxes are:

1. Moulinié Ainé boxes are known with Langdorff tune sheets endorsed Moulinié Ainé

2. They display all the "Langdorff Characteristics"
3. They fit in with Langdorff Numbering, see Table 6.

I think the weight of this evidence is enough to make the case. Similar evidence, but with fewer examples suggests that Langdorff also made for Malignon and for (or with) Henri Metert who was his partner from 1844 till 1852. They were all close together, in Geneva.

The implications for Langdorff are quite formidable. Think of the tremendous praise often heaped, justifiably, on the musical boxes of Malignon

Table 6. Giving a sequence of serial numbers, and cylinder end cap markings of Gamme and year, on musical boxes with the "Langdorff characteristics." All key wind except No. 13645. Attribution is stamped on bedplate, or noted on tune sheet, or both.

Serial No.	Attributed to	Marks on cylinder end cap	Cylinder length inches	No. of tunes	Type
1409	H. Metert	G16-44	8	4	F-Piano
1696	H. Metert	G179-44	12¼	6	F-Piano
1849	Moulinié Ainé	G448-44	11¼	4	F-P overture
2328	Moulinié Ainé	G419-45	9	4	F-Piano
2683	H. Metert	G232-46	13	6	F-Piano
2856	H. Metert	G391-46	11	8	standard
3919	Langdorff	G136/48	11¾	4	F-P overture
4171	Moulinié Ainé	G248-48	13½	6	F-Piano
4217	Malignon	G356-48	13	4	overtures
5192	Malignon	G185-50	13	-	-
5264	Malignon	G290/50	13	6	F-P & bells
5280	Malignon	G266-50	8	4	standard
6157	Langdorff	G550/51	15*	6*	F-Piano
6622	Langdorff	G431/52	13	6	F-Piano
6882	Langdorff	G602/52	13	6	Hidden D & B
6959	Langdorff	G715/53	-	-	-
7625	Langdorff	G113/54	9	4	Hidden D & B
7667	Malignon	G151/54	20	6	Pt overture
7785	Langdorff	G302/54	-	-	-
11258	Langdorff	G641/58	15½	4	F-P Mandolin
13645	Langdorff	G36/63	13	4	F-P overture

*interchangeable cylinders.

Early style.   **Later style.**

Fig 3-16 Two styles of marking on the bass-end cylinder caps of movements manufactured by Langdorff.

and Moulinié Ainé—all this praise almost certainly belongs to Langdorff! Now who says Nicole boxes were the best? Not that it matters, all the boxes made, certainly up to 1880, were so consistently good.

The marking on the cylinder end cap has so far been seen in two styles, as illustrated in Fig. 3-16.

Lecoultre Craftsmen

Craft finesse in a musical box can be the work of either the original craftsman or a dedicated repairer. Occasionally one can prove it to be the original work, as I have found on some Lecoultre boxes where all the comb screws are coded in Roman figures between the head and the screwed portion. I need hardly add that these markings had been overlooked or ignored by previous repairers and the screws were not in their correct order.

I have found these markings on a box with comb stamped LB for the Lecoultre brothers at Le Brassus, which is about half way between Geneva and Ste Croix, and I wondered if their craftsmen had so marked the screws. Then along came a hidden-drum-and-bells box with the comb stamped LF/Gve in a lozenge, for the Lecoultre brothers at Geneva, and it had exactly the same Roman figures filed on the comb screws. The chances of these two boxes having both been through the hands of the same subsequent repairer must be nil, so the markings must be original, and they link the Lecoultres yet again. There is also a nice piece of superfinesse on the bell box; it has one screw for the 16-tooth drum comb, nine screws for the music comb, and again one for the 16-tooth (8 bells) comb. The two screws for the small combs are shorter than the others, to avoid fouling the felt stop brackets. So the craftsman did not bother to code them, but he subtly coded the nine music comb screws from II to X. Such finesse from the 1850s is rather a delight, thought I must say in this case it borders on the fastidious. Perhaps only one of the craftsmen found this extra task for an apprentice, because not all Lecoultre boxes have these marked comb screws.

L'Epée

The L'Epée factory at Sainte-Suzanne, in the South of France near the Swiss border, started up in 1839 and was well established by 1845. It was very much on its own compared with the Swiss makers who had a network of component suppliers; and L'Epée decided to be self-sufficient from the start, though he wisely kept close to the traditional Swiss design.

The main distinctive features of L'Epée movements are their U-shaped steel click springs; wooden handles on iron winding levers; and polished, tin-plated cast iron bedplates. These bedplates were finished by a common and cheap process of the period known as "whitening," and consisting of tin plating over a flash of copper, giving a neat, polished, silver-white surface. Not surprisingly after a hundred years the tin gets attacked in places exposing patches of copper and sometimes patches of rust on the iron; these defects have provoked several inaccurate descriptions of the original process. The bedplates can be restored either by polishing down to the iron surface or by having them commercially re-plated . . . still over copper, but nowadays the tin is deposited by electro-plating.

L'Epée cases also generally have three distinctive features—the glass of the glass lid slides into its frame; the control lever platform is screwed to the upright; and often the mechanism is secured by bolts screwed into the bedplate legs through the bottom of the case.

Movements in these cases were sold by agents including A Woog and S Woog, whose initials were sometimes stamped in an oval beside the serial number on the bedplate. The tune sheets were often plain and headed "Musique de Genéve," a title which was the recognised description of this unique type of music but was naturally considered unnecessary by the Swiss makers.

L'Epée also sold movements with and without cases as the main supplier to Thibouville-Lamy of Paris, who did not manufacture musical boxes despite the suggestion on their tune sheets that they did. In France and in Switzerland it was usual to add *Fabrique* or *Fabricants* (namely that you had a factory or were a manufacturer) despite never making the item so labelled.

In giving these guidelines to L'Epée characteristics it must be admitted that the total number of boxes seen is far, far less than an adequate statistical sample. Also, some details may have been established only after L'Epée had been in operation for several years. For example Dr. J E Roesch in the 1974 Silver Anniversary collection of the MBSI describes details of eight L'Epée boxes, unfortunately without giving their serial numbers, and *inter alia* reports . . .

1. In all eight boxes the male Geneva peg was a steel pin fixed axially into the spring arbor. (I have seen this version on only one L'Epée box serial No. 1216, but I have seen it on a late Ami Rivenc.)
2. Only one of the eight had the wooden winding knob.
3. Four had tune indicators of a distinctive type with a curved pointer having very wide arrow-head.
4. Six had steel damper pins, one had brass dampers.

All eight movements and cases also conformed to the details given at the start of these notes. I think the damper pins were iron rather than steel, and it seems probable that most L'Epée movements originally had brass dampers, — not a good idea as they wore out along the track of their contact with the cylinder pins as can clearly be seen on any survivors. Dr. Roesch also made the excellent point that the U-shaped click springs were a standard type for French clocks.

All these features except the tune indicator and the pin type of Geneva stop are to be found on L'Epée serial No. 26925 with 16¼ inch cylinder and 74-tooth comb playing twelve tunes. See Fig. 3-17. It still has a few brass dampers (with iron pins) but of course they may not be the originals. They are from 0.013″ to 0.015″ wide. The tune spacing is 0.018″, compared with the general Swiss standard of 0.017″ which explains why there are only 74 teeth for a 16¼ inch 12-air cylinder. For these L'Epée move-

Fig 3-17 Tinned iron bedplate of L'Epée Serial No. 26925 showing S. Woog initials in oval and the characteristic wooden-handled winding lever.

ments the comb teeth formula has accordingly to be altered from 60 times to 56 times the cylinder length in inches divided by the number of tunes.

The twelve tunes on L'Epée No. 26925 are a good selection of mainly operatic airs, but the arrangements are rather pedestrian and some have stereotyped *finale* or make-length chords at their ends. All have excellent bass support, helped by good sound radiation from the 24½ by 7½ inch case whose sound board has a periphery of 60 inches. Rigid fixing of bedplate directly to soundboard probably also helps. Arditi's *Il Bacio* is very well done though it suggests rather a heavyweight kiss. *Wiener Kinder* is by Josef Strauss, opus 61, 1858.

All the L'Epée features (again excepting the tune indicator and Geneva pin but still with most of the iron damper pins) are also to be found on serial No. 40804, 9¼ inch cylinder playing six tunes with seven bells. The 73-tooth music comb and 7-tooth bell comb occupy about 8¾ inches of the cylinder which has wider than usual margins. The bedplate has no legs but a small semi-circular extension each end to take a screw into a wood block in the case, which is extremely ornate with extensive marquetry and brass

Fig 3-18 Ornate case made by L'Epée for Serial No. 40804, with brass legs, brass moulding around plinth and lid, elaborate cross-banding, and domed lid with large cartouche of brass, ebony, and enamel.

stringing on the front, sides and domed lid and was undoubtedly made by L'Epée. This No. 40804 has a green Thibouville-Lamy tune sheet.

Several L'Epée movements have been found with Nicole à Genève stamped on the bedplate. At one time this was thought to have been a fraud, cashing in on a well-known name; but it now seems far more likely that they were supplied by L'Epée to Nicole, probably to alleviate a temporary shortage. They have not (so far) been widely enough reported to confirm this or to sort out the origin of their serial numbers, though these are almost certain to be L'Epée's, those seen including Nos. 10349, 16295, and 17101, all lever wound.

Nicole Freres

Nicole Freres of Geneva, founded in 1815, gained an enviable and deserved reputation in England particularly due to their efficient office in the City of London and its consistent advertising (See Appendix).

This has led to the incorrect impression that Nicole was the best of the

80

Swiss makers. But, in reality the quality from all the leading makers is indistinguishable.

Nicole Freres ceased manufacturing musical boxes about 1880 at serial number about 48,000. The Company restarted as a sales and repair business in London about 1880 with a "Branch" in Geneva, and thereafter sold boxes with serial numbers above 50,000. Some of these could have been made in the Geneva "Branch," but certainly the majority were made for them by good quality makers, as yet unidentified.

Nicole dating

The accompanying chart, (Fig. 3-19), which is a plot of serial numbers against years, is my suggested ready-reckoner for the manufacturing dates of Nicole boxes up to the closure of the Geneva business in 1880.

I think it incorporates all published fixes, and no amendments were suggested when I showed it at our London meeting on December 12th, 1981.

The shape of the curve is characteristic for almost every enterprise;

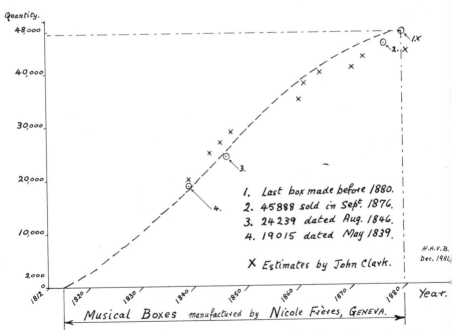

1. Last box made before 1880.
2. 45888 sold in Sept. 1876.
3. 24239 dated Aug. 1846.
4. 19015 dated May 1839.

X Estimates by John Clark.

H.A.V.B.
Dec. 1981.

Musical Boxes manufactured by Nicole Frères, GENEVA.

Fig 3-19 Chart connecting Nicole serial numbers with dates of manufacture.

lower output at starting, maximum output during hey-day, and a tailing-off towards the end. It is surprising how quickly the output accelerated; but this is strictly a chart of serial numbers and we cannot be certain that every serial number meant a box actually manufactured or that the numbers ran in strictly numerical order. Also, there may have been many smaller boxes in the early days.

The maximum rate of output, about 1000 a year, was achieved from 1830 till 1860, or even later if the shut-down occured earlier than shown.

Paillard

The Paillard family made significant contributions to the design and quantity manufacture of musical boxes, and so naturally the name crops up throughout any musical box history.

Fig 3-20 Several makers supplied the large 1890s market for modest multicylinder machines. This machine is a typical nickel-plated example, with three 9-inch, eight-air cylinders housed in the plinth drawer. Serial No. 217, maker unknown, but Victoria emblem in case suggests Abrahams. It has zither, tune indicator, and safety check.

They started production in Ste Croix during the 1840s and in 1875 built the first stage of an extensive new factory. Professor Chapuis in writing about the Ste Croix makers states that, "The Paillard firm alone produced 10,000 cartel boxes in one year," though this may be an exaggeration.

Paillard movements are most often seen marked PVF (Paillard, Vaucher, Fils) and they tend to have colourful tune sheets with the design often incorporating a simple white cross on red shield. They cover a wide range of types, from large individual specials to numerous 6 inch cylinder interchangeables. It is thought that they also made movements as subcontractors to agents and to other makers, including Nicole for serial numbers above 50,000.

Their very large output may have given the impression that PVF movements are not in the top quality league; but all the larger and special Paillard boxes I have seen are equal to the best contemporary standards.

Ami Rivenc

I think there was far more interchange of ideas, musical arrangements, subassemblies, and even complete cylinder musical boxes than is generally realized. For example, it is almost certain that Ami Rivenc made complete musical boxes for Bremond as well as for Dawkins, for selling under their own name, and by other agents. Their trade-mark was the winged lion, copied from part of the Brunswick Monument which was built in Geneva in 1874. They generally applied this trade-mark to their tune-sheets, and sometimes stamped it on the governor cock and sometimes also applied it as a stamped impression under the case, near the serial number.

The Bremond tune sheet illustrated in Fig. 3-21, serial No. 29290 and dated probably between 1875 and 1880, is a common type regarded as exclusive to Bremond because of the white cross above the lyre at top centre. But, with this box comes a slight shock when you look for the Bremond monogram on the governor cock and see instead Rivenc's winged lion! Could it be a substituted governor? But no, turn the box upside down and there is the serial number and again the winged lion, here rubber-stamped on the bare wood in purple. Illustrations of both are reproduced in Figs. 3-22 and 3-23. So without doubt this box was made by Ami Rivenc for Bremond, and the only real puzzle remaining is, whose is the serial number? Either the full No. 29290 or the abbreviated No. 290 appears stamped or scratched on the winding handle, great wheel, cylinder

Fig 3-21 Typical Bremond tune sheet for Serial No. 29290, with white cross above lyre at top centre. Size 8¼ by 5¼ inches, black on white, elegantly inscribed.

Fig 3-22 Ami Rivenc's winged lion trademark stamped on the governor cock of Serial No. 29290.

84

Fig 3-23 Underside of Serial No. 29290 case, showing the winged lion of the Brunswick Monument in Geneva. It was used as a trademark by Ami Rivenc, presumably, from 1874 when he began working on his own and, incidentally, when the monument had just been erected.

end cap, both combs and, in the usual bold writing, on the cast iron bedplate under the combs. So I think Bremond simply adopted the Rivenc serial number.

Another Bremond box made by Ami Rivenc has serial No. 19024 and the same type of Bremond tune sheet, but with a Rivenc maker's plate screwed to the lid above it.

Sallaz & Oboussier

No one seems to know whether these good people were makers or agents, but, I think almost certainly makers as several untraced smaller firms undoubtedly cashed in on the musical box boom of the late 1860's in Ste. Croix. They were powerfully aided by the ready availability of all types of component parts and by knowledgeable local craftsmen including tune arrangers; and anything they could not get locally could quite easily be got in Geneva.

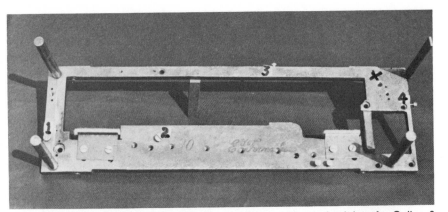

Fig 3-24 Underside of the Edmond Fornachon cast brass bedplate for Sallaz & Oboussier Serial No. 2126. (1) and (2) are screws holding the bell gantry, (3) and (4) at edges are drum bracket screws, and the arrow X indicates the screwed hole for a support leg which had to be replaced by the prop in the back right corner. Screw (1) is on the extension to the undersize casting.

The decidedly casual writing, spelling and spacing on this tune sheet are said to be characteristic of Sallaz & Oboussier, and here they have included the serial number but omitted to mention that this box has what we now call hidden drum and bells.

The whole movement is of good quality, with 112 teeth in the music comb, and it looks like similar Langdorff movements except for signs of uncertainty in both mechanism and case. The brass bedplate has the foundry code and name cast in—10 Ed Fornachon—but it was 9mm short at the treble end which was made good by a soldered and screwed extension. The left back supporting leg was positioned to go straight through the drum and was therefore replaced by an iron strip screwed to the edge of the bedplate. The serial number is stamped in the conventional left back position and R2 is stamped under the comb alongside three scratched Nos.—Gme 254; 26 (end of serial number); and 2 (an assembly number). The Nos. 26 and 2 are repeated on several components. The full serial No. 2126 is scratched on the three combs and governor and on several drum and bell details. As usual the gamme No. 254 is scratched on the bass end cylinder cap. The great wheel is stamped No. 2127—an adjacent serial number! I have seen this error before, presum-

86

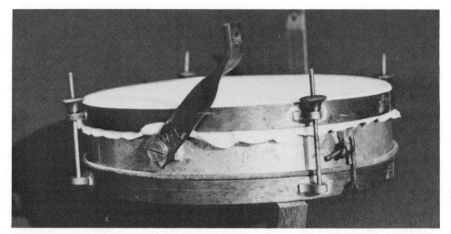

Fig 3-25 The Serial No. 2126 drum—fine vellum with four stretchers on both top and bottom, the latter with snare consisting of stretched catgut tied over a hook each side, as shown.

ably caused by an accident to the correct component forcing a substitution, not uncommon in manufacturing industry.

Everything about the music comb (stamped T near the centre) and about the 12-tooth drum comb and 15-tooth bell comb is conventional except that the tooth at the bass end of the bell comb is not only a dummy (no cylinder pins in its tracks) but has been added as an afterthought by soldering, edge-on. It overhangs the brass base of the comb and it presents an extremely neat soldering job. There is another unpinned track between the drum and music combs but no extra tooth was added to mask this so there is an unsightly gap.

The nest of eight bells is conventional but the drum is unusual, see Fig. 3-25.

Drum and bell boxes playing only four airs are very rare and the main reason for this is probably the fact that the tooth spacing of 0.068″ for four airs is very close for bell and drum teeth which, with their soldered legs, are a more practical proposition at a spacing of one tenth of an inch which corresponds to six airs. In this movement there are two blank, unpinned, wasted tracks for every one of the bell and drum teeth, see Fig. 3-26.

The cylinder is 11½ inches long and of unusual diameter 50mm (just under 2 inches). It has 4211 pins—music 2915, bells 453, drum 843, all

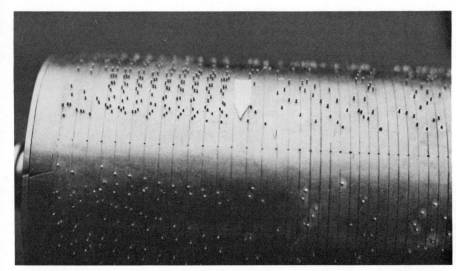

Fig 3-26 Bass end of the Serial No. 2126 cylinder showing the twelve wide drum tracks, then an unpinned track marked by arrow, then two wide and two intermediate bass tooth tracks before the start of the normal-width four-air tracks.

conventionally raked. The large quantity of drum pins is explained by the many drum rolls, which are exuberant but not strictly either necessary or musical. They are easily turned off to suit the older listener. Several of the setting-up dots along the tune gap on the cylinder were drilled right through and so had to be plugged during repinning; and there was no trace of the usual local set of dots indicating the intermediate tunes.

There are also unusual features about the case, which is of the early lever-wind type with hinged glass lid covering the full width except for the three control levers at the treble end. Instead of the usual little wood strips to support the glass lid when closed there were simply two iron sprags, which had certainly left their mark. The lifter was fixed to the top of the glass lid frame, looking unsightly and hard to let go compared with the conventional fixing under the frame which allows the lifter to unwind clear at the end of the lift. The usual partition over the spring barrel is not provided and the brass on-off lever is bent just above the bedplate to engage directly with the stop arm tail. A final rather unusual feature is the fine brass stringing around every piece of the kingwood, enamel and mother-of-pearl central scrolling design on the lid.

Change-over Panic?

Think of the repercussions among musical box case and component makers, when it became obvious, perhaps too suddenly for comfort, that the customer would no longer put up with the old-fashioned key-winding.

Nicole Freres seem to have taken the change very calmly, and spread it over at least two years. Despite their large output it is rare to find a Nicole box with any intermediate arrangement between their usual key-wind and lever-wind types.

But a bit of panic seems to have struck the Lecoultre brothers, as illustrated by the hidden drum and bells box mentioned below. They converted the mechanism quite neatly by shortening the key arbor and mounting on it a lever with ratchet. This of course was very close to the end of the case so the handle on the lever turns to the right as in many early lever-winds. The three control levers under the bed plate were replaced by three of Nicole type sprung against a brass plate mounted on a robust wooden mount sliding in the old key compartment grooves.

There must have been quite a number of such conversions, because the winding lever and handle are an integral brass casting, and I have seen two different types. So far so good, and incidentally the fact that the conversion was done in course of manufacture is confirmed by the mechanism serial number appearing on case components such as the mount for the operating levers and the glass lid.

Glass Lid Arrangements

It is in the glass lid arrangement that one sees the slight signs of panic. Late Lecoultre key-wind boxes had hinged glass lids covering the mechanism and sometimes also covering the key compartment; and hidden drum and bells boxes also had a narrow fixed section behind the glass lid, usually consisting of a wooden frame carrying perforated or patterned wood or card. The trouble arose with this narrow fixed section because in the converted box it fouled the winding lever. So they hinged it to the back of the case. It was already hinged to the glass lid so the result was a floppy double-hinged affair, only too likely to sag in the middle; and I think it did well to survive, almost intact, until its current restoration.

By the early 1860s almost the entire musical box industry had standardised on the separate compartments for winding lever and operating levers, with the glass lid neatly between.

Case Histories

There are several examples of a distinct though unreliable connection between the cylinder musical box makers and the cases fitted. In addition to the vertical front veneering for Conchon quoted above, Graham Webb has come across examples of Conchon boxes with the lid marquetry including both his trade marks—the angled ovals as seen on some governor cocks and the rather angular lyre which accompanied a five-pointed star on his letter headings.

One comes to associate Bremond boxes with superior lid and often front marquetry, having finer than average detail and more colourful woods or enamels.

More severe in style, with wide ebonized bands framing lid and front and sometimes also the sides, and with amboyna type veneer and inlay usually limited to a small display of brass and mother-of-pearl, comes a characteristic range of cases including those with matching tables. This style one associates with Baker-Troll—and, subsequently, with G Baker & Co. They often have a plinth, with added feet.

The only personalized glass lid lifters I have seen are on Baker-Troll boxes. They are of thin leather, embossed in gold with their monogram —T between normal and reversed B.

The Great Exhibition

Items on show in the Great Exhibition of 1851 tell an interesting story about what are now the antiques of that period. The official reports run to five hefty volumes, over 1200 pages each and containing some top class engravings. The text is very brief on exhibits but includes comments on current industrial affairs and procedures.

The exhibits were predominantly British, so it is not surprising that many notable foreign manufacturers did not exhibit—Nicole Frères for example. The only non-Swiss musical box exhibit was by Rzebitschek; that was the official spelling, British printers were not keen on adding "a whole lot of fancy accents" at that time. Thus:—

162 RZEBITSCHEK,F,PRAGUE—Manufacturer. Four musical boxes, playing two, three, four and six tunes.

The number signifies the 162nd Austrian exhibitor. All the headings differentiate between manufacturers and inventors.

The extensive Swiss entry covered a wide range from watches and instruments to textiles and textile machinery and chocolate. There were eight musical box exhibitors, and no one exhibited both musical boxes and watches. It was 1851, remember.

26 E. & A. PAILLARD BROTHERS, Sainte Croix, Canton of Vaud—Manufacturers. A musical box—Mandoline. Musical snuffboxes, playing respectively two, three and four tunes.

27 JACCARD BROTHERS, Sainte Croix, Canton of Vaud —Manufacturers. Musical snuff-boxes, in horn and tortoiseshell, silver mounted, playing two, three, four and six tunes. Another box, playing four overtures.

32 LECOULTRE, D., & SON, Brassus, Canton of Vaud—Manufacturer. A large musical box, with two combs, playing the following overtures, *viz*, De Semiramis by Rossini; Robert le Diable by Meyerbeer, and Guillaume Tel by Rossini.

33 JAQUES, LOUIS, & SON, St. Croix, Canton of Vaud—Manufacturers. Musical boxes, playing respectively 8 tunes, with forte-piano; mandoline, 4 tunes; 6 tunes, with drum and cymbals, 4 tunes, with castanets and cymbals; large size, 4 overtures, with forte-piano; mandoline, large size, 4 tunes, with forte-piano; two small, 4 tunes; two small, 3 tunes; six small, 2 tunes; and one, 6 tunes with forte-piano.

77 DU COMMUN GIROD, Frederick William, Geneva—Manufacturer. Musical boxes, carved and marquetrie.

83 GAY & LUQUIN, Geneva—Inventors. Complicated musical box, imitating a military band, plays six modern tunes, the barrel is nineteen inches long, and three inches four-tenths in diameter; it contains also harmonic tones, a drum, two castanets, twelve small bells, and a large drum, which are not seen; with a carved box and moveable glasses.

90 LECOULTRE BROTHERS, Brassus, Canton of Vaud. Musical box, plays four overtures, with two key-boards. Musical pianoforte, plated box, inlaid work, and glass.

97 METERT & LANGDORFF, Geneva—Manufacturers. Musical boxes, playing six tunes, with bells and drum at pleasure, ebony and black cases; musical boxes playing four tunes, mandoline, black case, all with metallic incrustations.

Swiss thinking in 1851 on accurate machining for interchangeability is exemplified by Antoine Lecoultre who exhibited various pocket chronometers including "Six movements, without escapement, with this peculiarity, that after being taken to pieces, and the pieces mixed, they can be placed together again, taking each piece as it presents itself, with the exception of the barrels and indexes and the screws".

Light Relief From a Polyphon

The penny-in-slot Polyphons featured by many pubs in the early 1900s had coin drawers measuring at least 9 by 5 by 3 inches deep. They could hold about 960 pennies—£4—though I should be very surprised if they ever got so full. However, there is no doubt that the bottom of the drawer was often well covered by coins, perhaps including halfpennies optimistically, but vainly inserted.

The presence of these coins caused the distinctive sound, about halfway through the tune, of "hearing the penny drop". So I am rather pained to have seen, in certain of these coin drawers, bits of cloth and even scraps of carpet laid in to deaden this famous sound—often quoted by youngsters who have no inkling of its origin.

Luckily there are still masses of old pennies around to work these machines and to line their drawers, and it is worth remembering that the price of 1d per tune was not particularly cheap in, say, 1910 when the price of a pint was 2½d.

These machines are wonderfully robust, and one sees them with bent winding handles, undoubtedly caused by athletic imbibers who became frustrated by the slower passages of tunes like *Cavalleria Rusticana*. Someone must have tried making a penny slightly sticky so it would traverse the chute but refuse to tip out of the coin tray. If the penny hasn't dropped, the machine is still playing.

Coin-operated cylinder musical boxes are very rare. They were too quiet, too delicate and too limited in repertoire for exploitation in public places.

4

CONTEMPORARY SWISS SCENE

What were communications like in Switzerland in 1830 to 1850 during the growing-up period of the musical box industry in Geneva, Berne and Ste Croix? Here are some key dates . . .

On January 1st, 1849, the Swiss Franc was adopted as the national currency: previously there was no unification of Cantonal currencies and different moneys and values totalling nearly 300 different coins were in legal use. Of course the watch-making industry must have got well used to this, as it was established in the 16th century and flourished specially in the Cantons of Neuchâtel, Vaud (for Ste Croix), Berne and Geneva.

In June of 1849, postal rates were fixed federally; previously the Cantonal posts were autonomous. But these rates were still based on both weight and distance, the former in steps of ½ loth (= ¼ oz) and the latter in four zones—up to 10, 25, 40, and over 40 leagues (1 league was a "road-hour" of about 3 miles). For local mail these rates were prepaid with the Cantonal stamp introduced in 1843.

In April 1850 Swiss Federal stamps superseded the Cantonal issues and the country's postal system soon became simplified and fully-fledged. Prompt action by the Cantons made Switzerland one of the first countries to follow the UK's introduction of postage stamps; they were several years ahead of their neighbours France, Germany and Italy. In August, 1851, a ¼ oz letter from Geneva to Ste Croix, about 100 kilometres cost 15 centimes or rappen and a 1 lb parcel, the maximum weight allowed, cost Fr 1·70.

The railway from Geneva to Yverdon (8 miles from Ste Croix) was opened in 1858 and extended to Neuchatel in 1869. The branch line to

Fig 4-1 Steam locomotive with snow-plough, and a group of skiers, at the Ste. Croix Railway Station.

Ste Croix, which made a big detour to cope with the climb of 2,000 feet, opened in 1893, steam hauled until 1945.

It is hard to visualize the huge output of musical boxes from Ste Croix in the 1880s going by road to Yverdon and sometimes to Pontarlier, ten miles away over the French border. Winter in Ste Croix brought conditions which nowadays cause panic among road users.

Feet, Thumbs, Lines and Points

These were the Swiss units of length, twelve of one adding up to the next bigger so you could take quarters, thirds and halves throughout, thereby upstaging the decimal system. The units were very close to our feet and inches (and our obsolete lines) and one pouce (thumb) equals 1.066." They persisted in Switzerland and to a lesser extent in France long after the metric system was established in 1801. Some musical box manufacturers used them right into the 1890s to record cylinder dimensions on

94

Fig 4-2 Business as usual in the market place, St. Croix, November 1900.

their tune sheets. But if you measure such cylinders you will very seldom find that their overall length tallies with the nunber of pouces stated.

There are three possible interpretations of cylinder length,—the overall length including end caps, or the length of the barrel, or the length of the actual playing, pinned surface. It is the last of these which I have found most commonly tallies with the pouces stated, and I think this is very logical of the Swiss because it fixes the main dimensions of a musical box, namely the effective lengths of cylinder and comb. It rightly ignores additional unused lengths where a cylinder is longer than its comb or vice versa, both these cases being fairly common.

Naturally there were exceptions, and I have seen Thibouville-Lamy boxes with cylinders distinctly shorter overall than the pouces claimed on their tune sheets, an exaggeration which persisted right into the period of their innumerable small nickle-plated movements housed in large cses.

In sharp contrast I have seen a P.V.F. tune sheet actually stating the cylinder length as "7½ inches." Its cylinder measured 8.125″ overall and had a pinned length just over 7.9". Perhaps they simply got their arithmetic wrong.

In the comparatively rare cases where the diameter is also given, it is expressed in lignes of which 12 went to a pouce. Far the most commonly seen on tune sheets is 24 lignes = 2.132" which is a shade over two and one eighth inches. One could almost call this the standard cylinder diameter.

L. G. Jaccard, 1861-1939

The Jaccard articles, written in 1938 when the author was 77 and reprinted by the Musical Box Society International, are both fascinating —and tantalizing because they could have been so much better. Jaccard joined the musical box industry in or near Ste Croix when he was 16, in 1877, by which date as he records most variants of the cylinder musical box had already appeared. Yet, to give just one example, he describes both Mandoline and Tremolo types as having "many prongs tuned to the same pitch", but fails to make it clear that they are merely different names for the same effect. Of his apprenticeship years he is frustratingly short of vivid detail, and I must confess that I simply do not believe his claim that (in 1877-78) all musical boxes, "had all their cylinder pins bent forward, one after the other, in order to place them in their correct position according to musical notation to make the different notes of the chords fall together in perfect unison." What did he really mean when he wrote that? It is necessary to challenge obvious error, lest it be added to the strings of traditional errors repeated by writer after writer.

Jaccard is at his best and most valuable in recalling the names and expressions obviously long accepted in the musical box trade by the time he joined it. They were so obvious to him that he never thought of explaining their source. In cold fact, all cylinder movements with the spring arbor perpendicular to the bedplate which were first made for snuff-boxes, were simply called Snuff-boxes (Tabatières). The others, with spring arbor parallel to the cylinder, were first made for clocks and were called Wall Clocks (Cartels). I must say I have not previously seen the latter explained, the French noun *cartel* now being restricted, in its second meaning, to antique wall clocks.

Two other French nouns in the articles possibly merit translating; *Gabarit* means large scale model. And *Manivelle* means (wait for it) crank-handle. No one would accuse these name fixers of letting their imaginations run riot.

Jaccard's interesting statement that "With my father I interviewed many masters of the craft, each a specialist in some particular line of the industry, and sought an apprenticeship with one of them. . . ." seems to be definite proof that any detail of a musical box could be obtained from one or other small specialist craft workshop. Presumably one could hire the services of a tune arranger and then order up every detail needed for a new musical box. Such must have been the birth of many of the legion of unidentifiable boxes.

Alfred Chapuis, 1880-1958.

Professor Chapuis was a distinguished scholar and historian whose many published works covered horology, history, and fiction, including plays. His 1955 book, *History of Musical Boxes and Mechanical Music* is very good on history and on general descriptions, but disappointing on technical detail of cartel musical boxes. His descriptions of manufacture (which was in its heyday when he was born in 1880) reads like vague recollections of the past supplemented by examples of later procedures, particularly as regards pinning. His pinning illustrations show very small and very late type cylinders being worked on, and comb production is covered by two similar views of a small comb being tuned from a 75-tooth master. It all sounds romantically complicated, particularly the statement that every one of the 4,800 to 6,000 pins in a six-air cylinder was individually raked and verified for accurate performance. Everybody who has repinned a few cylinders will know that this is not necessary; that only a very few pins go awry; that there is always the occasional unmarked pinning error; and that, contrary to this acount, pricking and drilling errors are comparatively infrequent.

Chapuis goes on to say that the zither is put on last and that the mechanism is generally held in place by three screws through the bedplate legs; but neither of these features was known in Switzerland before 1880. Very wisely and interestingly he covers part of the repair procedure by quoting a paper written by Ami Rivenc in 1876 which is concise and lucid.

The book contains numerous pictures of musical boxes of most types, but the types are not classified and, disappointingly, no tune sheets are reproduced nor are any serial numbers given.

Both Chapuis and Henry L'Epée (in the MBSI Silver Anniversary collection) state that a certain cylinder after drilling could be used to reproduce as many similar ones as required. They do not explain how this was done, or the size limitations, or the date of inception. Presumably it only applied to small cylinders and was done on copy-drilling machines which became common in manufacturing industry in the 1890s. It certainly was not used in the "golden period" during which every cartel musical box was unique.

The lasting value of these writings rests mainly with their fascinating overall picture of an astonishingly local industry which achieved well merited international renown.

5

TUNE SHEETS

Tune sheets (more correctly, but hardly ever, called tune cards) are the only documents spanning the long lives of musical boxes. They are, so to speak, birth certificates and even when quite badly damaged I think they should be rescued and restored—using the methods explained in Chapter 8.

Unfortunately many makers failed to identify their tune sheets and, worse, several makers not only used very similar types, but changed them haphazardly over the years. Moreover, many agents and some firms which never made musical boxes added their names in ways which implied that they were the makers.

As more and more tune sheets are definitely attributed to known makers, the chances of correctly replacing missing tune sheets are increased. Many replica sheets are now available.

Identifying all the tunes usually involves some patient research,—and some help from Musical Box Society members.

Often, there is a regrettable lack of information on tune sheets, and yet extreme irritation can be caused by those gratuitous additions to them which are often carelessly scrawled and in anachronistic blue ink and of dubious accuracy. A neater solution to the problem is to prepare a separate card, sized to fit neatly beside the winding lever or in the key compartment, and on it to write . . .

1. Details of the musical box.
2. Additional notes for each tune, and
3. (On the back) *your* name, dates of purchase, repairs, etc.

What additional notes? Well there are three things people often like to know about the tunes, namely . . .

1. Nationality and life span of composer
2. Source and date of each tune
3. Comments.

You will be rather lucky if all this information is readily available, so leave room to add items that come to hand in the future. If you recall how fascinating it is to find and read an apt comment written a hundred years ago, you will be spurred on to adding such notes. For example, if your box plays *Toi que l'oiseau* from the opera *William Tell* (first performed 1829) by Rossini (1792-1868) it is worth noting that this tune is now better known as *The Scottish Soldier*.

Several musical box makers used tune sheets decorated with two gar-

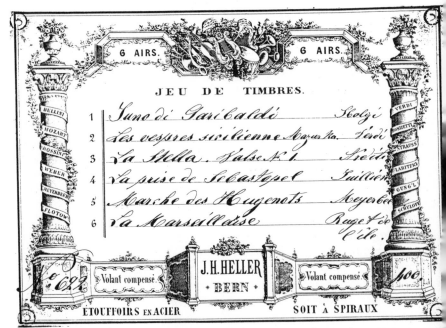

Fig 5-1 One of the many tune sheet designs with an array of composers, seen with many minor alterations in the design and used by several makers. This sheet by Heller for Serial No. 1076 with 10¾-inch cylinder and six bells.

landed columns around which were entwined scrolls carrying the names of famous composers. Spaces were left for the number of airs, and for headings such as *Jeu de Timbres*, and for a serial number, and sometimes a maker's name such as J H HELLER of Berne, and occasionally a technical claim such as *Volant Compensé* (balanced governor); and often the common though long obsolete announcement *Etouffoirs en Acier— Soit à Spiraux* (spiral steel dampers) . . . by 1865 this was analogous to writing "four wheel brakes" on a modern car.

An interesting anomaly with these composer-embellished tune sheets is that many of the tunes played were not by the named composers. And a tantalizing feature of all tune sheets (in addition to their sometimes fugitive nature) is their casual approach to tune listing. They seemed to set out with the best intention of listing the three relevant items, namely the source work, the individual tune, and the composer; but it is rare to find that they persevered to the end. A famous air from a Bellini opera may be listed as *Norma* or as *Casta Diva* or, correctly as *NORMA—Casta Diva*. The composer may only be named for some of the airs—and this with a nonchalant disregard for his degree of eminence. There are also some frightful spelling mistakes, though admittedly these are very few when you consider that the source material was a mixture of Italian, French, English and German, and that the writer was usually a French-speaking Swiss.

Several makers of cylinder musical boxes must have produced more than a thousand per year; but even at 500 a year involving, say, four different types or sizes of tune sheet their 6-months ordering level was about 6 dozen. If they ordered a gross at a time they would still be liable to run out of certain types at least two or three times a year; and one sees clear evidence of this in the use of tune sheets with their printed number of airs altered, and with too many tunes crowded in for the size of sheet. What one does NOT see evidence of is the occasion when, say, D Lecoultre & Son ran out of cards and nipped smartly down the road at Le Brassus to "borrow" a few from Lecoultre Freres,—("Not again!") This must have happened at times—and with so many makers so astonishingly disinterested in tune sheet publicity, why not?

This disinterest is confirmed by similar cards being commonly used by different makers, though probably these makers were more closely allied than records show. I think the printers simply offered their standard designs, sometimes making minor changes on request.

This vague situation, so puzzling today, was compounded by the same printers supplying several makers. For example A Haas with works at Ge-

Fig 5-2 Tune sheet of Lecoultre Frères Serial No. 36766 with oval shaded panel near top left in which the serial number is normally written as shown. It is hard to believe that the same careful hand which wrote the tune titles also carelessly ran into the margin when adding tune details. The agent's monogram is at bottom centre; the Gamme number is lost in the leafy design to the right of it,—G 136. Tune No. 4 is not the second, but the fourth part of the *William Tell* Overture, namely the final galop.

neva and Mulhouse supplied at least Langdorff, Conchon and Bendon. Then again there must have been some competition between printers, because some makers switched their custom. Did any printers send out samples, and were they ever used, thereby adding another red herring?

It is slightly surprising that some patterns of tune sheet persisted in use with very minor modifications for three decades. More persisted, I think, than can be explained by occasions when a few old tune sheets were found at the back of a drawer, and naturally enough put to use . . . even, if they dated from an earlier ownership of the company or had been borrowed from friends down the road.

So, tune sheets are highly unreliable as date fixers.

Also, there are two reasons to be suspicious about the numbers, generally taken to be serial numbers, quoted on tune sheets. Sometimes the serial number was abbreviated by omitting the first digit which from the maker's point of view only changed every 10,000 boxes, that is about every ten years. And sometimes the gamme number was written—probably by accident—in place of the serial number. For example, lever-wound Lecoultre serial No. 36766 is quoted on the tune sheet in Fig. 5-2, but key-wound Lecoultre serial No. 35373 has only the gamme number 8539 on its tune sheet, which is the same pattern. Both these boxes are those excellent 4-air, 5 inch cylinder, 72-tooth comb jobs so well done by Lecoultre with superior tune arrangements and often very plain cases. As a point of interest the gamme number of serial No. 36766 is 9136, so Lecoultre seem to have used up gamme numbers at a much faster rate than Nicole.

Some of the earlier examples of tune sheets with printed tune lists had their tune list printed specially just for the one box. The printing was mostly in gold and probably done by agents rather than makers. Presumably you could arrange by "special order" on the maker or agent to have words of your own choice added. An example seen recently on an unidentified make of box had a message in German printed below the list of tunes: "To our dear Emilie on her second birthday, September 25th, 1895".

Some tune sheets include and actually name composers long outdistanced by time and fashion. Four such appear, among their better-remembered contemporaries, on the tune sheet in Fig. 5-3.

This tune sheet is unusual in several respects, apart from the nationality spread of its named composers. It is rare to see, among the decorative cherubs, flowers and musical instruments along the top, a description of the type of musical box, here given as HARPE-ZITHER ACCOMPAGNE-MENT, though of course this merely means that a Zither has been added. Then again it is unusual to find a misleading heading above the tunes, here *Mandoline Piccolo*. This reads like a mandoline box with additional piccolo comb, whereas in fact it is not a mandoline main comb but the piccolo effect is spread over more teeth than usual and just about earns the label "mandoline".

The tune sheet is printed in red and gold and carries no clue to the manufacturer, nor for that matter to the lithographer. It measures 8½ by 6¼ inches.

The movement has a 16 inch cylinder with combs of 60 and 32 teeth and the bottom of the case, the soundingboard, measures 24½ by 8¼ inches so the bass notes can be strongly heard. They provide two dramatic moments in tune No. 4. The zither tissue covers all the main comb teeth except the eight lowest notes, but the tubular Nickel-plated tissue housing covers the whole main comb and an inch beyond. There is no am-

Fig 5-3 Made in Ste. Croix, but unidentifiable, Serial No. 5255.

biguity about the zither placing because it is screwed directly to the bed-plate and is not, as is more common practice, held by one or two of the comb screws. The tissue roll is secured via an iron rod inside the zither housing which is secured by two knurled brass nuts to the hinged zither support. There is no ambiguity about the length of the tissue which is indicated by two iron rods, an eighth of an inch in diameter, soldered inside the tubular housing to compress the tissue to an oval shape and so prevent it becoming too sloppy.

The spring controlling the zither is of unusual design. The brass wire spring carries an oval brass ball which slides freely in a hole in the hinged support and is sprung towards the cylinder. When the zither is in operation the ball is central in the hole, preventing rattle; when the zither is raised clear of the comb it is held in this position by the ball protruding through the hole and springing inwards. The two small set screws each side of the control knob allow a fine adjustment of the zither setting. See Fig. 2-8

The circle of cardboard inside the main spring housing of this musical box was cut neatly from a printed postcard calling a meeting of the Ste. Croix Town Council for January 13th 1878. I have cleaned and replaced

104

this interesting item! I think one can reasonably assume from it that the movement was made in Ste. Croix about 1880.

Almost everyone in the U.K. and the U.S.A. has heard of the ancient and classic tune *Yankee Doodle*. Its origin is obscure, though it was published in America in 1778 and a manuscript version is known dating from 1775. Numerous theories about its origin surfaced during the 19th century, prompting the Library of Congress to undertake an exhaustive enquiry into the subject. They completed their work in 1909 and their conclusion was that the origin of *Yankee Doodle* is obscure.

It has always been a popular tune and naturally appeared on disc— 15½ inch Polyphon 1805, 19⅝ inch Polyphon 5567, 15½ inch Regina 1578. But despite being current throughout their span of life it is rare on cylinder musical boxes which adds to the interest of the tune sheet reproduced in Fig. 5-4 where it appears as the (rousing) last tune. Also of interest is the polka credited to Schubert, whose works are surprisingly rare on musical boxes. But perhaps the most interesting bit is the maker's name,—see Chapter 3.

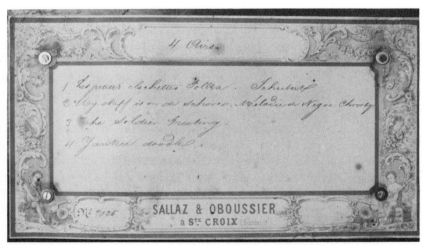

Fig 5-4   Strangely, this 180 by 100mm tune sheet, printed in blue, omits to mention its drum and bells. Serial No. 2126 is described in Chapter 3. Tune No. 2 is wrongly credited and Tune No. 3 is so similar to *Yankee Doodle* that it is an idiotic choice among only four tunes.

The Langdorff Mandoline Forte Piano tune sheet illustrated in Fig. 5-5 lists a strange mixture of tunes. The first is the *Krönungslieder* (= coronation songs) waltz by Johann Strauss II composed in 1857. Next is the often heard gypsy chorus from *Il Trovatore*, 1853. The "Melodies Valaques" of tune 3 are folk tunes of Wallachia, the country which joined with Moldavia in 1859 to become Roumania. Composer Edouard Wachman (1836-1908) was born in Bucharest and his wide range of works included a collection of local folk songs, as here played. Another folk tune turns up in the excellent "Triumphal March." This is by the Danish composer Peter Heise (1830-1879) and the basic melody of the march is practically identical with the nursery rhyme tune for *Baa Baa Black Sheep* which in turn is the same as a French tune, *Ah vous dirai—je Maman* the source of which is lost in antiquity among European folk tunes.

Three distinctly unusual tunes in a repertoire of four! It would be so interesting to know whether they were chosen by Langdorff or by a customer (or by a tune arranger).

Fig. 5-6 shows one of the later style tune sheets, probably a bit before

Fig 5-5 Langdorff made many Forte Piano boxes and this was usually noted, as here, at the foot of their standard tune sheet. Other special features, here Mandoline, were usually noted below the tune list.

Fig 5-6 Well into the cherub era with Serial No. 5941 of unknown make, a less common type of Harpe Harmonique Piccolo described in Chapter 2.

1885, from an unknown maker, but well decorated with musical cherubs, then in fashion. It has the serial No. 5941 written in the top margin and again among the cherubs just below the composers' names, and tunes from *La Mascotte* (1880) and *Patience* (1881) which Gilbert furnished with the alternative title *Bunthorne's Bride*.

The composer Emmett (1815-1904) is rare on cylinder boxes. Born Daniel Decatur Emmett in Ohio, he was a composer and performer of Negro Minstrel music and visited England in 1843. His other compositions include *I wish I was in Dixie's Land* (1860) and *Turkey In de Straw* (1861).

Figs. 5-7 to 5-25 illustrate a variety of tune sheets.

Fig 5-7 Baker-Troll tune sheet in sepia and grey-green for 16-inch cylinder Serial No. 15546 with BTB monogram obscured by lower left pin. Latest tune *La Cigale,* 1886. The cylinder is nickel-plated. Transfer in the case credits manufacture to "Geo Baker & Co (late Baker-Troll)."

Fig 5-8 Conchon tune sheet for Serial No. 3946, about 1870, with 9 bells in view, worked from separate 9-tooth comb. The first tune, usually translated *Wine, Women and Song,* was composed in 1869 and is the latest of the eight.

Fig 5-9 Large 10 x 7½-inch tune sheet of Bremond orchestral Serial No. 6329 with 19½ x 2-inch cylinder playing organ, six bells, and hidden drum and castanet. This time the garlanded columns honour twenty composers.

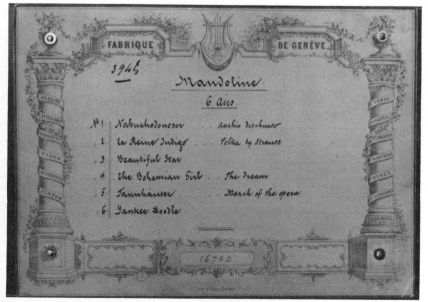

Fig 5-10 Back to twelve composers (Beethoven dropped) on this Bremond variant for Serial No. 16742 with 13-inch cylinder and 123 comb teeth. Latest tune from *Indigo*, 1871. The lyre at top centre is the less common type. The 394G written at top left must be the Gamme No., though it appears as 304 on bass tooth lead.

Fig 5-11 There are sundry minor misspellings on this tune sheet printed in gold presumably by Agent C. Scotcher for Conchon two-comb 14-inch cylinder Serial No. 7481. The zither is on the bass-end Mandoline comb.

Fig 5-12 Typical face-above-lyre device of Ducommun Girod here on Serial No. 1340 with 16¼-inch cylinder and, as stated, drum, 11 bells, and castanet.

Fig 5-13 Lecoultre Frères Serial No. 11484, with tune sheet carrying their initials top right and their agents' bottom centre. Top panel was altered in ink from TROIS to Quat for the four overtures played by 11 x 3⅛-inch cylinder on 158-tooth comb.

Fig 5-14 A common design printed in blue and here extensively repaired at the top, used by several makers and often by Lecoultre. This one is for Serial No. 23132, Gamme No. 4259 (noted on tune sheet) made at Le Brassus with 199-tooth comb stamped LB and giving the "super mandoline" effect.

Fig 5-15 This box of unknown make, Serial No. 28967, dates from the late 1880s - *The Mikado* was composed in 1885. It has a 13 inch cylinder with two 46-tooth combs in Sublime Harmonie arrangement. It uses the two combs to contrast loud and soft musical passages exactly in the manner of the Paillard patent. So, while it may justify the claim "Forte Piano Harmonique" it is definitely not a Forte Piano movement of the classic type.

Fig 5-16 This typical many-medalled green Thibouville-Lamy tune sheet, which clearly implies their manufacture, belongs to L'Epée Serial No. 40804, 9¼-inch cylinder with seven bells. The small note "Timbres en vue" not exactly emphatic. Both movement and highly ornate case made by L'Epée.

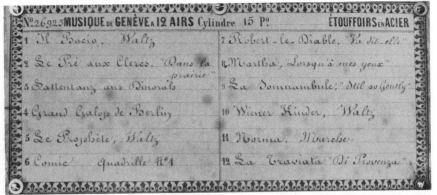

Fig 5-17 Musique de Géneve retained on a tune sheet commonly used by the French maker, L'Epée, for boxes sold through agents A and S Woog. Here it covers the 12 airs of Serial No. 26925, with 16¼-inch cylinder and 74 comb teeth. Bedplate is stamped SW, for S Woog.

Fig 5-18 The heading EXPRESSIFS on this early tune sheet for Lecoultre and Granger Serial No. 3493 describes what we now call "Single Comb Forte Piano," with 12-inch cylinder and 120 comb teeth. The note MUSIQUE de GENEVE became superfluous and was discarded, about 1840, by most of the Swiss makers.

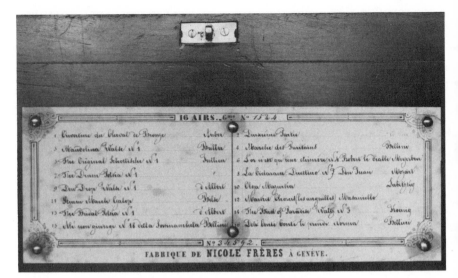

Fig 5-19 A double width tune sheet, unusual with Nicole, for Serial No. 34592 Gamme No. 1524, 19¾-inch cylinder. It plays 16 airs 2-per-turn. The first two are halves of the *Bronze Horse* overture; they run through without a break because a plug on the cylinder end cap protrudes into the stopping slot in the great wheel. The plug is withdrawn when the cylinder shifts to Tunes No. 3 and 4 and so the mechanism can stop after Tune No. 3.

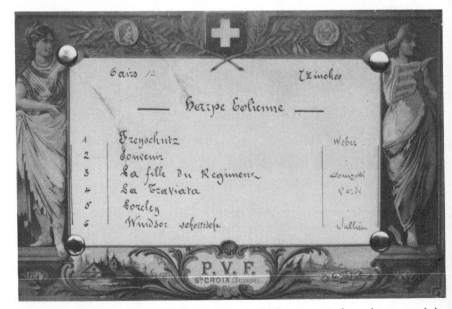

Fig 5-20 Typical coloured PVF tune sheet which seems to have been used, in many minor varieties, by C. Paillard and by Paillard, Vaucher Fils. This one is for Serial No. 1617, described in Chapter 2.

Fig 5-21 Another coloured PVF with variations. The black lettering has blue shading in Zither-Automatique and red shading in Mandoline Expressive.

Fig 5-22 This design of a coloured tune sheet, again with many small variations, is often seen on later musical boxes of unknown make. Many have their serial number stamped on the bass-end cylinder bearing bracket—as with this Serial No. 5044, 11-inch cylinder, two combs with 51 and 26 teeth.

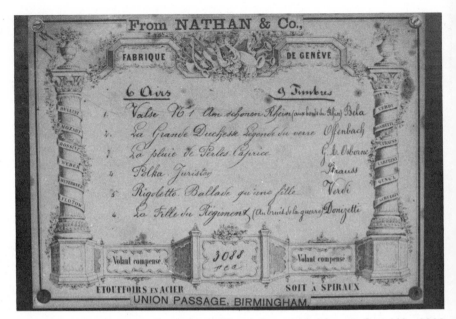

Fig 5-23 Though generally similar to Figs 1, 9, and 10, this unit, Serial No. 3088 with 11-inch cylinder and nine bells is unidentifiable. The tune sheet, mechanism, and the case—with above-average marquetry on lid and front—are all typically Bremond. However, there is no clinching evidence.

Fig 5-24 Another unknown maker's tune sheet, probably in the early zither period, for 17¼-inch cylinder playing 80 forte teeth with zither and 42 piano teeth. The Serial No. 959 is on tune sheet but 960 on movement. I have seen a similar tune sheet numbered 960 on a similar movement numbered 959. (How's that?)

←

Fig 5-25 Another unknown, and another variant on Fig 1, for the Organocleide described in Chapter 2. The tunes are well chosen to exploit the bass-mandolin sustained notes. Tune No. 5 is not the first but the third part of the *William Tell* Overture, namely the Pastorale *ranz des vaches*.

117

6

APPROACH TO RESTORATION

The restoration of a cylinder musical box—sometimes from a disconcerting mass of rust and verdigris in a battered box—is one of the most satisfying jobs in the whole field of antiques restoration.

It can now be done so well that the results would pass inspection at the long forgotten maker's works, just as it did well over a hundred years ago.

Quality Restoration

Everyone needs an occasional refresher, and what better refresher for an amateur craftsman than a careful look at the corresponding professional? So, I went gleaning to the craft works of Keith Harding, who kindly let me have a private session with some of his experts. They are undoubtedly expert, are really interested in musical boxes, and display a lively team spirit in criticism and help. Though one picks up numerous tips in such sessions, I will confine this report to their actual, current method of getting an overhauled box to play as it should and incidentally, to pass its final inspection by Keith Harding or Cliff Burnett, neither of whom like mediocre musical boxes.

Here is their procedure, starting at the point where the mechanism has been restored with a repinned cylinder, and the comb has been cleaned and any new teeth or tips fitted and all teeth accurately aligned for height and spacing, and old dampers all removed, but pins replaced as withdrawn.

1. Stone tooth tips to remove all signs of wear, thus restoring flat, square ends to the tips as viewed from below the comb. Great precautions are taken to retain the original chamfer angle at the tips, and to ensure that

all tips are perfectly in line—checked by viewing against a ground straight-edge.

2. Reset comb on bed-plate, adjusting dowels for correct lift of teeth. Extreme bass teeth to have about twice the lift of extreme treble.

These two operations are, frankly, beyond the normal capabilities of anyone who has not taken serious guidance in this type of craft work. Both require skill and patience, and tools beyond normal amateur resources. The fact that some people rashly press on regardless is unhappily proved by damaged combs, necessitating rescue work and retuning and sometimes even retipping, which ultimately reach professionals like Harding and Co.

3. Check synchronisation—bass and treble teeth intended to play simultaneously must drop off the cylinder pins simultaneously, so when extreme treble teeth are in line with the cylinder dots the extreme bass teeth must be below the dots by an amount equal to the treble end lift. To achieve this, one of the cylinder bearings may have to be raised a few thousandths of an inch by inserting a shim between it and the bed plate.

4. Insert about five dampers, and watch during play to see if their curve is ideal. For thinner cylinders and for combs sloped more steeply a flatter curve of the damper wire is needed. Try more dampers till the ideal curve is found.

5. Rule-of-thumb for position of end of damper: height above tip to equal tip width (which makes an easy at-a-glance check) and curve of damper, if continued, should just reach end of tip. Damper wire should be cut with sharp end-cutters, then there is no need to stone the cut ends.

6. Rule-of-thumb for damper wire size on average comb: .09/.08/.07mm for bass/centre/treble teeth respectively.

7. Feather dampers, for which goose feathers or thin parchment are used, are only fitted where found necessary.

8. Check all teeth for pitch and correct where necessary.

When all these jobs have been done correctly, there can still be undesirable noises such as:

(a) Wrong notes—caused by a bent pin or a new pin inserted by mistake in a deleted hole, or in an unmarked hole meant to be deleted.

(b) Pin noise, sometimes likened to bird chirruping, due to a bent pin rubbing the side of an adjacent damper or tooth tip: cured by applying trace of oil to extreme tip of pins with a glass plate smeared lightly with clock oil.

(c) Loss of quality caused by an error in the original piercing of the cylinder where all or some of the pins in part (usually last part) of a tune are slightly displaced. This was not common and can be spotted visually in the case of the tune pinned on the cylinder lines. Such pins are corrected by bending individually.

For the cosmetics of restoration these craftsmen strongly favour the traditional methods supported by improved modern materials. So they do all detail cleaning and polishing by hand using a leather-faced polishing stick with the ubiquitous Solvol Autosol. New parts and those damaged or corroded are first prepared using the three finest grades of Silicon Carbide ("Wet-or-dry") paper. This procedure closely copies the original finishes and is in line with the ethics of restoring antiques: the guiding principle is that the mildest practicable cleaning methods are used.

People like myself who spent most of their working lives in charge of production and engineering works tend automatically to look underneath work-benches for further clues. Here I found quite a surprise—a large pile of books most of which were the complete scores of music-box-period operas, including rarities like Meyerbeer's *Dinorah*. They are used assiduously and to excellent effect in replacing long-lost tune cards.

Another quality restorer who has helped me with second opinions on various oddments is Jim Colley of Southville, Bristol. He uses expert associates for restoration of cases, comb teeth, gearing, governors and disc machines, and himself handles cylinder repinning with a small team of pinners. He was very pleased when, during 1981, he chalked up his 250th repin.

His speciality is to achieve accuracy at the pin/tooth interface, and he emphasized the desirability of keeping the repinning wire diameter as close as possible to the original. Though one finds replacement pins of 0.015″ diameter—and on lamentable occasions even larger—he never exceeds 0.013″; and if the cylinder hole is too big he uses damper wire as a wedge. During recementing, the cement flows into the gap between the pin and the oversize hole producing a firm bond.

He is also very particular about checking comb tooth tips against their cylinder and resetting any teeth which may have moved slightly sideways, perhaps due to a run. Such teeth are liable to slip sideways off some pins and to interfere with pins of an adjacent tune,—both causing unwanted noises. Having achieved the ideal pin/tooth line-up, he removes traces of tooth wear by grinding, to restore the clean, sharp edges which produce a clear melody without stray noises. With badly worn combs this involves retuning at the treble end.

These good people were often pioneer engineers, and it will be extremely sad if they are upstaged by faceless electronic time-markers. They relish their own nomenclature, for example describing as "steady pins" what all engineers call dowels; and perhaps they enjoy mild swipes at ordinary engineers—I found in Britten's *Watch and Clockmakers' Handbook, Dictionary and Guide, 1907*, the comment "Engineer clockmakers invariably make their escape-wheels and other quick-moving parts too heavy".

This 1907 guide was published by E & F N Spon and contains under the heading "Musical Box", a 3-page entry similar to but much shorter than that reprinted from Vol III of *Spons Workshop Receipts*, 1909, in *The Music Box*,Vol 5, No. 8, Spring, 1973.

Britten's entry opens:

As nearly every country watchmaker is at some time or another called on to repair these instruments, a few hints thereon will not be out of place. It may be premised that, if a very large number of the pins on the cylinder are broken, the box had better be sent to an expert. But . . .

(and it concludes):

I have to acknowledge the courtesy of Messrs C Paillard and Co, who have readily answered all my enquires on the subject.

The damper illustration is identical with that on page 402 of the above-mentioned issue of *The Music Box*; but Britten advises filing a dove-tailed notch in the comb when fitting a new tooth, and "drive it tightly into position, and to make it secure, slightly rivet it or run a little solder into the joint by heating the spot with a blowpipe or heavy soldering-bit". Thank goodness a simple slot plus effective soldering is now found to be fully adequate.

Causes of Disaster

Most owners of musical boxes have vague fears of a 'run' and I hope such fears may be allayed by noting that responsible owners' experiences of a run are extremely rare. I have heard this fear expressed as 'the terrific pent-up force held only by a tiny gear wheel', whereas in fact the maximum load on a governor wormwheel with the spring fully wound is less than 1lb (450 grams) on a typical 13 inch cylinder box and should in fact be about the same for all normal boxes, the gear ratios being selected both to apply the extra torque needed for long and fat cylinders and to prevent overloading at the governor. It would take more than ten times this load to bend a normal wormwheel tooth. Measuring the load is easy, it is simply the weight needed to deflect the endless downwards.

Undoubtedly the most common cause of a run has been unwise tampering, mainly around the governor. If either the governor securing screw or the cock screw or the endless bottom bearing adjusting screw is loosened enough, a run is inevitable. Also, though the endless is designed with a shoulder to prevent it going out of mesh if the end stone is removed, a replaced endless or an altered top bearing could remove this safety feature in which case loosening the end stone plate screw would cause a run.

I think mechanical failures have always been very rare causes of runs. The only three examples I have gleaned from talks with experts comprise two failed repairs and one metal failure,—respectively a wormwheel inadequately riveted to its pinion which came adrift; an endless fitted with a new lower spigot which fell out; and a fractured pinion shaft.

Possibly some runs have been caused, directly or indirectly, by hamfisted or wilful winders-up coming up hard against the Geneva stop. One sees this on tormented boxes as deep scars on the female Geneva or the male peg broken off or the securing screw of the female sheared off . . . or sometimes all three. After that the ham-fisted can wind till he or she is only stopped by the spring anchor on the barrel, which one sometimes sees thereby distorted; and at a guess I think this might add up to ten times the normal maximum torque from the spring, with perhaps an added shock effect.

Runs can range from utter disaster, if they occur at full winding and with tunes set for change, to minor upset if the spring is nearly run down and tunes set to repeat. So a pessimist leaves his musical box always set to repeat!

Surprise is sometimes expressed that a bad run seems to knock cylinder pins over in both directions and to cause gouging of the cylinder surface. This is because the heavy cylinder accelerates to a high speed and its momentum carries it past any stopping position after which it will reverse before coming to rest. At high speed and not being balanced it will in places pass closer to the comb. If set at tune change it will undergo rapid sideways movements. Also during the run some pins and teeth and tips are broken off and some are likely to jam between comb and cylinder.

Eye-Glasses

Young children's eyes focus down to 5 inches or less; they see small things wonderfully big and one notices them painting and drawing with their chins almost touching the paper. When adults first need glasses they usually get them for reading at a distance of about twelve inches. But at this distance some musical box components look exceedingly tiny, so one invests in a variety of magnifiers of which the most useful is the type which hinges to normal spectacles and can therefore be swung out of the way when not needed. But, it is always a bit tiring to work with one eye even when, as advised by all opticians, the other eye is relaxed by being kept open. Binocular magnifiers never seem to be as satisfactory as expected.

For various good practical and theoretical reasons opticians (in my experience) are not keen to prescribe "reading" glasses to focus closer than 5½ inches; but I have found it well worth having a pair so made. They enable you to dispense with the magnifiers for almost all musical box jobs and being fully corrected they are easy on the eyes. The only discipline needed when wearing them is always to keep the eyes at the prescribed distance from the work.

Before Dismantling

Before dismantling a musical box for cleaning or restoration it is very well worthwhile to check over all moving parts and list any improvements needed.

First, while the mechanism is still in its case, do all the controls work correctly? Do the wooden partitions fit firmly in their grooves? Are the spacers between the bed plate and the case sides thick enough to prevent distortion when the case screws are tightened? It is obviously better to make and fit new ones before repainting or polishing the bed plate. And are there any strange buzzing noises, indicating sympathetic vibrations from something loose? Cleaning will not cure them so they are well worth tracing and fixing.

Second, the mechanism itself,—are the winder click springs set strongly enough? Does the Geneva stop-work run sweetly without binding or rattling? Is the tune change engagement OK? Does the tail on the end-

123

less engage the stop arm cleanly, giving instant stop without stuttering? Is the stop lever spring strong enough? Does the tail run free of the stop lever throughout a tune? Occasionally one finds the groove on the great wheel is not perfectly concentric, which causes the tail, if set too fine, to tickle the stop lever at one part of the tune, making an irritating noise. It is unwise to bend the tail while the governor is mounted on the bedplate because this introduces a slight risk of breaking the endless and a considerable risk of loosening the tail.

Armed with the above data one can make the necessary small adjustments while cleaning the components and, with a bit of luck, get everything working correctly first time, after reassembly.

Chamber of Horrors

With the present cult of horror shows, may I walk you round an assembly of horrors which I have noted down (with shaking hand) as perpetrated on musical boxes. I have numbered the exhibits in case anyone can surpass them.

1. Nine bass teeth glued together between their leads with a powerful oil/dirt mixture, flattening all their associated cylinder pins.
2. Broken tooth "invisibly" repaired by gluing a strip of steel under it.
3. Six new teeth fitted, but of full width right to the tips. They all played every tune simultaneously, an unusual effect.
4. Lead weights attached to the wings of the butterfly.
5. Jewel plate soldered to governor cock.
6. Tune card, already long overdue for major repair, reaffixed to lid with patches of thick glue.
7. Control lever partition of a lever-wound box glued into its slots.
8. Loose brass inlay on case refixed with two large carpet tacks.

I only make passing reference to wood worm and to discs which so often seem to have been stored in damp cardboard; and I merely continue to wonder why all music boxes coming up for restoration have *all* their screwhead slots damaged, presumably by wild screw drivers.

It is well said that one person's horror is another's joy, so, my last exhibit asks a question—is this really a horror? I think it is.

9. A modest 6 inch cylinder 3-bell box with large case which has been painted all over in pale blue.

7

MECHANICAL RESTORATION

Pin Straightening

Cylinder musical box restoration almost invariably involves straightening some bent cylinder pins, and the tedium of this job can be reduced by evolving an "ideal method." I prefer the cylinder cleaned but not highly polished and mounted on its arbor, with snail cam and drive pin removed, between two wood blocks with V-notches screwed to a firm base.

I first check the rake of the pins, in strips about half an inch wide along the full length of the cylinder. Teeth with incorrect rake usually stand out clearly from their neighbours and are easily put back into line. If some seem to be slightly wrongly raked I leave them alone, the error is very small. Only if there is a widespread lack of uniform raking is it worth setting up the cylinder in a lathe and reraking, and this should only be done after straightening any pins bent sideways. What an Irishman might describe as an overwhelming minority of cylinders have non-raked, radial pins and these are treated in just the same way. Pins which have been knocked right over by a serious run or other ill use almost always break off during straightening and if in quantity they call for a repin.

Before starting to straighten any pins bent sideways, an examination of the whole cylinder will usually show that the majority of pins which are not perfectly straight all lean slightly in the same direction, usually towards the treble end. Then obviously the only pins needing attention are those leaning in the opposite direction and those leaning excessively. This approach saves a lot of time and indecision, I have found, and it is helped by having a clear idea of the acceptable tolerance, which I have indicated on the accompanying large-scale drawing, Fig. 7-1. Unless the pins are consider-

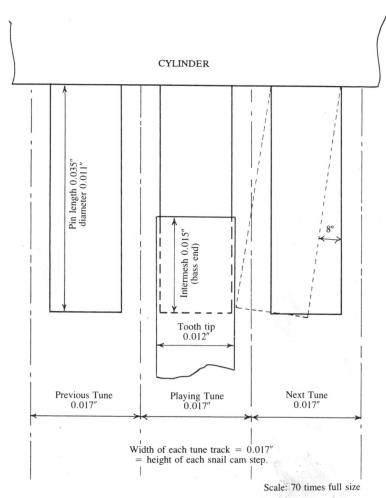

CYLINDER

Pin length 0.035"
diameter 0.011"

Intermesh 0.015"
(bass end)

8°

Tooth tip
0.012"

| Previous Tune
0.017" | Playing Tune
0.017" | Next Tune
0.017" |

Width of each tune track = 0.017"
= height of each snail cam step.

Scale: 70 times full size

Fig 7-1 Plan view of typical cylinder musical box comb/cylinder interface, with tooth tip and cylinder pin sizes with clearances. The adjacent tune pin shown dotted indicates the maximum permissible sideways bending before interfering with teeth playing another tune.

ably longer than 0.35", which is unusual, there can be a total angular variation of 16 degrees before interfering with adjacent comb teeth. In practice this excessive variation would cause trouble by pins sliding off worn teeth and fouling imperfect dampers; but a range of about 8 degrees is tolerable

126

and quite easily attainable during straightening. This figure keeps all pins within their tune tracks. If all the pins are either straight or leaning in the same direction, the norm would be those leaning perhaps 2 or 3 degrees and the cylinder would be set up so that these were central with the tooth tips.

I do the straightening in bands not more than half an inch wide, rotating the cylinder a few times for each band with a white background, so that one can see the lines of pins for each tune and quickly spot any pins sufficiently out of line to need attention.

Tools

A blue-ended hypodermic needle cut down to about half an inch and with 0.012″ diameter wire threaded through to expel any pins that break off while straightening. Cut the needle with wire inside to prevent squeezing.

Marking

Blue or purple felt tips show well, and clear marks save a lot of time by eliminating duplicated effort.

Viewing

A 4 inch focal length lens of the type that clips onto one's ordinary glasses. Use eyes alternately and shield the eye not in use so it can be kept open, as all opticians advise.

One of the great attractions of musical box music is its delightful clarity, and this largely depends on the accuracy of the cylinder pins.

Tune Track Width

The tune track width can be calculated very accurately by measuring the effective overall length of the comb and dividing this by the number of teeth multiplied by the number of tunes. By effective comb length I mean from the first tooth tip to the end of the tooth spacing just beyond the tip of the last tooth. The answer is astonishingly constant, at 0.017″, give or take a few tenths of thousandths. Equally astonishing is the fact that this important dimension is not a simple fraction of a ligne, —nor for that matter of a millimetre. The nearest is one fifth of a ligne = 0.177", but this would have been unthinkable to the Swiss who had a duodecimal system and reckoned 12 points to a ligne, so 2 points = 0.015". But whatever produced the 0.017" dimension, all makers kept in line and my experience to date is that the track widths are all exactly the same for any one maker and that they differ by less than a thousandth of an inch from one maker to another. This strongly suggests that they all had their own home-made machines for cylinder pricking and comb teeth slitting; famous machine-tool makers like SIP of Geneva only started up in 1862.

The fact that 60 times 0.017" = 1, near enough, made possible the easy ready reckoner:

$$\frac{60 \times \text{comb length in inches}}{\text{Number of tunes}} = \text{No. of comb teeth}$$

Strictly, "number of tunes" should read number of cylinder revolutions to complete the tune programme, which for example would be eight for a 24-air 3-per-turn movement. Many boxes with fine combs playing only 3 or 4 airs have a number of bass teeth wider than average to allow them sufficient weight, and this involves a corresponding number of unpinned tune tracks, so the formula does not apply.

Repinning

It is rather irksome though in no way difficult to remove the cement and the pins from a musical box cylinder, but in the subsequent repinning operation I have found several items of interest. The cylinder I have just finished repinning is 14 inch long by 2⅛ inch diameter and belongs to an 8-air mandolin movement with ten bells by Bremond, No. 17614. It had one or two peculiarities—only the treble end cap was pegged to the barrel and that, unusually, by only two brass pegs. Also the inside surface of the cement was very uneven with two considerable bulges, suggesting some handling before it was properly set. Both these items rather suggested a previous repin. But on the other hand the two internal dividers, though rather badly placed, had been drilled into and there were no signs of damage at the corresponding pin holes. Also there were no notches indicating the orientation of the end caps, which are almost always emphasized by repinners: the bass end orientation was indcated by two centre dots on the cylinder surface corresponding with two dots on the face of the end cap, and the treble end orientation depended solely on the two peg holes. All this shows once again how hard it is to distinguish definitely between original and restored work. Incidentally the orientation of the bass end cap only matters when, as in this case, it is cut away in places to clear pins in the end tracks.

Dividers

One or sometimes two dividers (rather strangely so called) are fitted in longer cylinders to prevent distortion. They are usually about ⅛ inch (3mm) thick, chamfered to half that thickness at the periphery, bored about 1 inch diameter, and made of brass or zinc. Zinc dividers, often made from castings presumably as an economy measure, have to be removed because the acid would dissolve them before starting on the steel pins. The makers probably inserted the dividers (and fitted the end caps) before pricking and drilling the cylinder and undoubtedly some makers took more trouble than others to place the dividers in scantily-pinned tracks.

Both the cast Zinc dividers in this Bremond cylinder fractured during extraction, the castings were very coarsely crystalline and comparatively brittle. Both had been placed near, but not at, the least-pinned tracks, so both had been drilled to receive about twenty pins. The depth of drilling into them was about 0.02," about ½mm, giving adequate anchorage.

The two end caps had presumably been drilled into just enough to mark them so that clearances for those pins could be filed. This considerable extra work was obviously thought justifiable to save about 5mm on the cylinder length.

I made two new brass dividers and I also claim a noteworthy technical improvement by scalloping the periphery with 16 semi-circular slots made by a ¼ inch round file, each about 0.2" across leaving between them 16 lands each also about 0.2" long to bear on the inner surface of the cylinder. This scalloped divider is a trile easier to insert and is twice as easy to keep clear of cylinder pins, as I found by pinning the tracks astride them first—I could adjust the dividers slightly till they interfered with no pins. I took care to make the new dividers the same diameter as the end cap fitting, and certainly no bigger; one sometimes winces to see cylinders with humps where a strong-arm restorer has forced in an oversize divider.

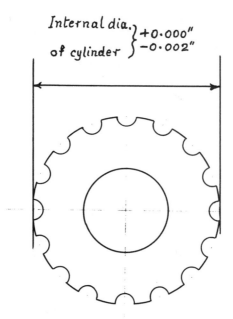

Internal dia.⎱ +0·000"
of cylinder ⎰ −0·002"

Fig 7-2 Scalloped cylinder divider made from brass not less than a sixteenth-of-an-inch thick and tapered to about half of that dimension at its periphery.

The Re-Pin Operation

I have found a surprising variation in the time taken for the actual insertion of all the new pins. Some cylinders accept the same diameter of wire in, say, 98% of the holes—as did this 14 inch Bremond. Others need two or even three sizes, which can more than double the time taken assuming brute force is never resorted to. But in addition to this variation, all cylinders I have met have had one or two per cent of damaged and oversize holes—due I imagine to previous errors and attempts to insert single replacement pins. Some of these holes are merely oversize, some are surrounded by small pits where the brass has been struck or gouged, possibly to close in an oversize hole. My advice for dealing with these (from a tip first given to me by Jim Colley) is to keep to the wire diameter used for the majority of holes and to wedge it into these oversize holes using a fragment of the thinnest available damper wire,—preferably inserted at the

130

leading edge of the hole so as to keep the pin central in its track. If you take a short length of damper wire and bend the last 1mm to a sharp right angle it is easy to insert and hold in the pin hole with one hand while the other inserts the wire. After driving in the pin the damper wire is easily broken off flush with the cylinder. It may be necessary to cut the damper wire to one-half width if the pin is hard to insert.

Recementing

To prevent fouling the edges of the cylinder while ladling back the cement I fit thin aluminium protectors made quite roughly from (second-hand) small foil food dishes, by cutting a hole in their base about ⅛ inch smaller than the cylinder internal diameter. The big advantage of scalloped dividers is that with them you need not be too particular about getting the correct amounts of cement in each section between and beyond the dividers because the cement will find its own level along the whole length of the cylinder (assuming your lathe bed is horizontal!) I like to have a small tell-tale hole in one or both end caps situated at what will be the final internal diameter of the cement filling, and I plug all other holes. Heating can safely stop a minute or so after traces of cement have appeared at the tell-tale. This Bremond cylinder needed a 30-minute cooling run, the first five minutes fan-assisted. I have found a speed not less than 300rpm advisable, to ensure that there will be no messy traces of cement on the cylinder arbor, which I also grease as an added precaution.

I have found an astonishing variation in cylinder cement, ranging from very thin and runny to a sort of sandy porridge. Sometimes there are quite large lumps in it, and sometimes two colours where, presumably, a re-pinner has had to top up. All types have (so far) given me the same smooth satisfactory glossy surface within the cylinder. But this cement is a very poor conductor of heat so a large quantity takes a long time to heat or cool right through. Heating at too high a temperature does not hurry it, but merely drives off some of the solvent thereby reducing its quality and providing a formidable smell.

If is important to examine the cemented cylinder closely for bent or pushed-in pins; the latter are easily pulled back after gentle local heating with a fine-flame burner.

Grinding and Setting

I use a fixed stone for grinding, and the main precaution here is to ensure that the final two or three thousandths of an inch are ground off with a fine stone and not more than a thousandth per pass, to ensure that no 'rag' is left on the leading edges of the pins. All grinding dust should be cleaned off and a heavy oil applied freely to the cylinder before pin setting.

I have found 0.0035" the ideal interference for pin setting; but however carefully done I always find up to about 2% of the pins bent sideways—though not all bent enough to interfere with an adjacent tune track. Straightening in the case of this Bremond cylinder took about two hours in half-hour sessions.

It is always an exceptional pleasure to hear a repinned cylinder playing, with all the missing notes, and in this case two complete tunes restored. The only outstanding chore is to decide which pin to delete where there are two too close together. It takes patient listening, helped here because the four cases were all on the same tune. I think it is usually the later pin of such pairs that is correct, the earlier one being more likely to have been pricked first, in error, and its delete mark omitted; but repinners more expert than me disagree with this possibly facile assumption. All agree, however, that a repinned cylinder plays better after all the tunes have been played a few times.

I advise anyone embarking on repinning to start with a cylinder not much longer than 6 inches, and preferably one free from damage around the pin holes. I was encouraged to start by Graham Webb's book, and the procedure I have followed, then and now, is that of Keith Harding's *Musical Box Workshop Manual.* The Bremond 14 inch cylinder has 6250 pins for its 91-tooth music comb and 9-tooth bell comb (the latter playing ten bells, the treble pair from one tooth). In one pouring wet May day, and without overlong sessions, I put in 1100 pins,—which might seem slow to a professional, given a cylinder with such consistent hole size. It took me about 6 hours. Looking back at the several cylinders I have repinned over the last few years, my only regret is failing to find any clues to the sequence of the pricking operation. All the errors seem to be completely random. The most bizarre I have seen is on a 10½ inch Henriot cylinder No. 11544 where, about two seconds after the end of the first tune, there is a nice little chord of three notes. But this chord does not occur either at the beginning or at the end of any tune on the cylinder! And these three stray pins are not deleted. I left them in as a tribute to some 1850's craftsmen who nodded thrice.

Cement

Melted cylinder cement goes through a plastic stage while cooling, during which it can be moulded to shape almost as easily as chewing gum. So the question naturally arises—at what temperature can the cement be relied upon to retain its rigidly solid state?

This is difficult to answer with the many different (and seemingly casual) cement mixtures that were used; but there is one indisputable fact, namely that this cement can and does flow, albeit very slowly indeed, at temperatures as low as 110°F = 44°C, and probably in some cases at even lower temperatures.

Depending on the summer weather in the British Isles, these temperatures are met for a few days or a few weeks every year in most attics and in most south-facing windows and certainly in out-buildings. Therefore anyone leaving a cylinder musical box for longer than, say five years in such conditions should note that there is a very real danger of cement flowing. Even if the box is only sometimes placed in these hot spots it merely extends the time, because the effect is cumulative and is concentrated on account of the cylinder always being parked in the same rotational position. Imagine what can (and does) happen in hot climates.

In extreme cases the cement flows enough to foul the arbor and prevent tune changes; but usually, on looking into the cylinder, one sees a slight wave of cement the full length of the cylinder emerging from what should be a neat circle. The resulting out-of-balance can also be diagnosed with the cylinder assembly alone on the bedplate, because it will always come to rest with the heaviest part at the bottom—which is usually the normal end-of-tune position. With a 3 inch cylinder the out-of-balance effect can be quite dramatic. By the time it has got near to fouling the arbor the cement may have sufficiently denuded some cylinder pins to cause a loss of sound quality while they are in play. Don't even think about what happens if the box suffers a run under these conditions.

A cylinder 13 by about 2 inches in diameter rotated at about 350 revs per minute requires about fifteen minutes heating to redistribute the cement, using a fish-tail burner on a small blow-lamp traversed slowly back

133

and forth along the cylinder with the tips of the blue flames about an inch from the rotating surface. Then it must be left rotating for about a further 35 minutes to be sure the cement is fully set.

Have a chat with someone accustomed to repinning before doing it for the first time, because several precautions are necessary, particularly in setting up the job on a lathe and in subsequent cleaning of the arbor and cylinder. During the cooling run, air reenters the cylinder and by the time it is cool this new air will have deposited moisture which will rust the arbor bearing surfaces if not thoroughly cleaned. How does the air get in? Between the arbor and the end cap bearing holes which are very far from being hermetic seals.

Comb Finesse

Before starting any work on redampering it is worthwhile, after cleaning the comb and mounting it on a wood base, to insert under the teeth a piece of thick white paper about an inch wide along the centre of which a dot can be marked for every tooth tip, with a larger dot for every fifth one and a numbered line for every tenth. On this paper can be noted the successive damper wire sizes, and any problem teeth. After redampering it is useful for pin-pointing any teeth which do not play correctly.

Next, decide which, if any, of the existing dampers are in suficiently good condition to retain—i.e. correct shape, free from kinks, free from rust, firmly secured, and with unimpaired springiness. If the answer is less than about 25 per cent, it will almost certainly be quicker and better to replace the lot. Fig. 7-3 is a reminder of the correct damper shape.

Place packing washers between comb and wood base, and sound each tooth in turn so as to identify any which may be out of tune. Tuning is helped when the pitch changes are scratched on the comb base, but even without this aid it is comparatively easy to hear a faulty tooth because either it does not quite match an adjacent tooth or it mars the musical progression up the scale. It may simply be that a damper pin is missing; if so, fitting a new one will restore pitch. The effect of the damper wire is only significant at the extreme treble limit of wire dampers. The amount of weight affecting tuning is proportional to the total tooth weight, so one can be careless about damper pin size at the bass end of the comb, but elsewhere any oversize damper pin will lower the pitch of a tooth, a common cause of minor tuning imperfection. When two or more teeth are of the

134

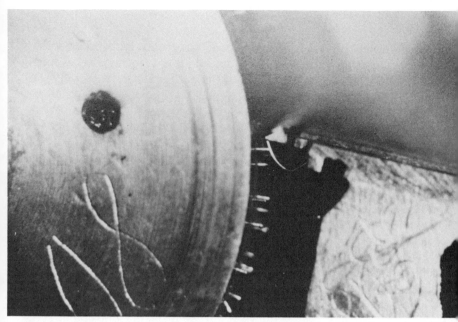

Fig 7-3 Seen from the bass end, a cylinder pin (radial) just touching a correctly-shaped damper.

same pitch, exact tuning can always be comfirmed because if one is sounded the other will vibrate in sympathy, which can be discerned if the tooth is touched with a pin.

Where most of the existing dampers are good enough to retain, it is worth making a special tool for sounding the teeth. Take a few inches of steel strip about 1/16 inch wide by about half that thick and file one end to an L-shape. The base of the L is inserted sideways between damper and tooth and pulled forwards and slightly downwards which sounds the tooth with no risk of straining the damper and is handy for immediately touching an adjacent tooth to check sympathetic vibrations. It is also good for cleaning the undersides of the tooth tips.

The final job before redampering is to remove all relevant damper pins and, before replacing them exactly as found, making sure that all fragments of old damper wire are cleared from the holes. For this the best tool I have found is a twist drill of the appropriate size held in a pin chuck. The day before removing damper pins I give them a shot of penetrating oil.

Tooth Tuning

Illustrated in Fig. 7-4 is a typical cylinder musical box tooth from near the bass end, complete with lead tuning weight. It is a steel spring which, if lifted and suddenly released, will vibrate at its natural frequency which depends solely on its geometry. The length AB is generally about half-an-inch and is constant throughout the comb, while the length BC carries the lead weight and diminishes towards the treble end of the comb.

Suppose for example the pitch of this tooth is too high. Then you can lower it either by reducing its thickness near the root, or by adding to the lead weight. Clearly therefore it is possible to alter the performance of the tooth without altering its pitch by both thinning near the root and *reducing* the lead weight. Doing so makes a tooth sound softer and more mellow. Conversely, a thicker tooth with greater lead weight gives a more bright or harsh sound.

This is not a wide-ranging choice. If the mellowing is overdone the tooth loses volume of sound, an effect demonstrated in fortepiano boxes as can be seen by comparing teeth of identical pitch on the two combs; that on the piano comb is the more slender and carries less lead. For the reason explained above the contrast between the piano and the forte combs is not as wide as many arrangers must have wished, and I think this explains the comparative demise of these boxes, which demand a sympathetic ear to appreciate their undoubted subtleties.

There is no difficulty or ambiguity in adding to or taking from the lead weight; but the operation commonly described as "removing metal near the root" involves in fact a choice of two entirely separate options, as illustrated, much enlarged, in Fig. 7-5. Either the tooth can simply be thinned near the root, or it can in fact be lengthened by decreasing the root radius

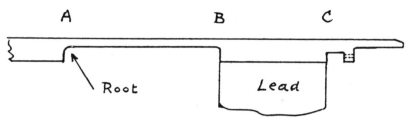

Fig 7-4 Standard design of a bass-end tooth, almost always made from spring steel ³⁄₃₂-inch thick.

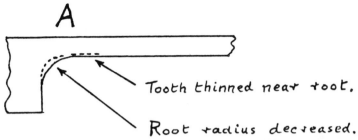

A

Tooth thinned near root.

Root radius decreased.

Fig 7-5 Lowering the pitch of a tooth. The preferred method is to lengthen the tooth by decreasing the root radius; because, any thinning reduces the stiffness so the tooth would play more softly for a given lift.

without altering the thickness: or, of course, a bit of both. I think the latter is the more desirable, as the former must make the tooth play more softly.

Presumably it was to allow scope to the comb tuner that some makers arranged a slight thickening of the tooth towards the start of the root radius; I have measured teeth 0.003″ thicker at A than at B, with most of this thickening occurring near A.

Another way of putting this is to say that the root radius runs out gradually in the first few millimetres of the tooth. It is in this region that one usually sees file marks, presumably made by the comb finisher or tuner. These file marks are often surprisingly rough, from a 2nd cut as opposed to a smooth file; and I must say that on a few occasions I have improved the ring of a dull tooth by such filing, though I cannot imagine why.

Comb Tooth Setting

Sometimes a run or other accident strains a comb tooth so that it is no longer in perfect alignment with its neighbours. This adversely affects both the playing of the tooth and the appearance of the comb. The old horological manuals gave the following remedial advice . . .

Place the top of the comb on a steel stake or anvil, face downwards, and to elevate a tooth tap the under-surface gently with the hardened peen of a hammer so as to stretch it. In the same way, if a tooth is to be turned to the right, stretch the left edge. If a tooth is to be depressed, an expert will bend it with a smart blow of the hammer on the middle of the underside while it rests on the anvil, but this is risky and will often result in a broken tooth. It is better to stretch the upper surface of the tooth with light taps, even though the marks show.

The cautionary note is apt, because anyone applying this sort of smart blow is liable to end up far more depressed than the tooth. It is only excusable if the striker knows the hardening and tempering history of the tooth in question.

I have obtained the same result more easily and with far less risk by simply bending the tooth back to its correct position. My method is to clamp the comb very securely and arrange a dial-gauge (or any reasonably fine measuring device) at the tooth tip. Then I deflect the tooth say a tenth of an inch and note that on release it returns to its original position. I then increase the amount of applied deflection, in steps of about 0.02″, until some permanent set is obtained. Then I reduce the steps to 0.01″ till enough permanent set has been applied to place the tooth exactly in its correct position.

How safe is all this? I acquired a broken bass tooth from a Henriot comb; it had fractured at the root so it was practically intact. With the broken end gripped in a smooth-jawed vise I found that a deflection of over 0.20″ was needed before any permanent set occurred. To achieve a permanent set of 0.005″ the deflection needed was 0.26″. This test reassured me, and of course it was more severe than if the tooth had still been on the comb, as about a tenth of an inch of its length was inoperable, being held in the vise. This tooth was very hard at the tip and right under the lead platform, but tempered towards the root where it carried the usual transverse file marks on its underside and where it would accept the small set needed. But any sharp blow near the hard part would inevitably cause it to break.

Damper Pins

Refitting damper pins is a job which I have found to vary from quite easy to exasperatingly difficult. The easy type is on a coarse ten or twelve-tune comb with well tapered and well fitting existing brass pins which can all be easily removed and reused. The most difficult is a 3-tune comb with very short and scantily tapered pins, particularly when they have been driven in too far to be pulled out and so have to be drilled and new ones made. It is even worse with iron pins which are harder to drill out and are seldom reusable.

These fine-tooth combs present a double problem—seriously reduced working space between teeth plus the need to use very small pins at the treble end to avoid lowering the pitch. Small pins can be very difficult to insert and it is rather daunting to be faced with fitting two or three dozen of them. Also, when new pins have to be made it is obviously helpful to know the ideal dimensions. Typical dimensions near the middle of a comb and hints about fitting can be gleaned from the accompanying drawings Fig. 7-6, which for clarity I have made 60 times full size and with the following dimensions:

Damper pin hole diameter	0.022″ (0.56mm)
Damper pin maximum diameter	0.022″ (0.56mm)
Damper pin taper	10% (i.e. 1 in 10)
Damper pin length	0.100″ (2.54mm)
Damper wire width	0.012″ (0.30mm)
Damper wire thickness	0.003″ (0.08mm)

The Fig. 7-6 drawing shows how the entry diameter is reduced from 0.022″ to 0.017″ when this damper wire is inserted. This is one reason why small damper pins are hard to reuse, previous damper wire often being narrower and therefore causing less restriction. The top right drawing shows the effective diameter at about 0.019″ after the pin has bent the damper wire to conform to its diameter. It follows, as shown on the lower drawing, that the maximum pin diameter need be no more than about the hole diameter. The minimum diameter of the pin must obviously be comfortably less than 0.017″ for easy insertion; alternatively the minimum diameter can be kept at 0.017″ and a small flat filed on the top of the leading end of the pin.

Some early movements had sharply tapered pins, tapering from a pointed end to about 0.025″ diameter in about an eighth of an inch. This is a taper of one in five, easy to insert but less reliable for gripping the damper wire, particularly in reuse. I think the ideal taper is about 1 in 10, so a typical pin would taper from 0.022″ to 0.012″ over its tenth-of-an-inch length. With 0.08″ damper wire it would protrude about 0.022″ which is adequate at the easier treble end and leaves scope for cutting off part of the thin end of the pin if necessary to raise the pitch of a tooth. But note that, if pin diameters are identical, a variation of 0.001″ on hole diameter (which is not uncommon) changes the protruding length by 0.01″.

The large scale drawing also shows how the pin grips the damper wire by its edges only, as it forces the damper to follow the pin radius which is smaller than the hole radius. This is in fact helpful as it reduces the stress

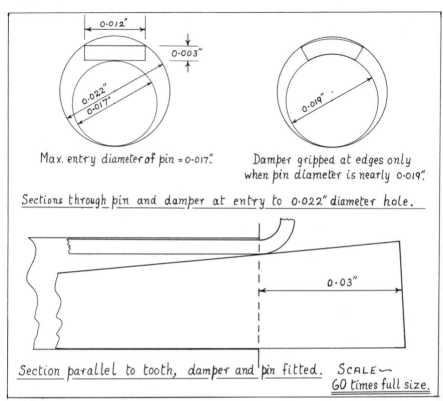

Fig 7-6 Large scale drawing showing how a damper is gripped by its pin.

on the wire when it is bent upwards before shaping. Even so, a sharp bend upwards will cause cracks at the edges, and the stress raising at these points explains why old dampers so commonly break off just there. If a new damper is accidentally bent sharply upwards during fitting, it is certain to crack and should be replaced.

To minimize these stresses and to aid insertion, damper wire should obviously be as narrow as practicable, and I think the ideal width is between 0.009″ and 0.010″. Current supplies are around 0.012″ and 0.013″ which is undoubtedly too wide and has the further two disadvantages of impeding pin insertion and being more likely to interfere with the cylinder pins of the adjacent tunes if insertion is a bit inaccurate.

The force needed to insert the pin tightly enough to hold the damper wire firmly depends mainly on the taper; more force is needed with a sharp taper and so light hammering-in is generally necessary. The ring of a tooth is impaired if a damper and pin are slightly loose. The edges of the damper pin hole are sharp and hard, and very often a burr is thrown up on the pin; this burr should be removed before a pin is reused.

A damper in operation has the properties of a cantilevered rectangular bar, that is to say its stiffness is proportional to its width and to the cube of its thickness. The latter explains why the common range of damper wires, in 0.01mm steps from 0.06 to 0.09mm, is effective, the stiffness increments being broadly constant. Thus for example though the 0.08mm wire is only 14% thicker than the 0.07mm it is 1½ times stiffer; and again the 0.07mm is just over 1½ times stiffer than the 0.06mm.

Soldered Dampers

Circumstances certainly alter cases, a good example being sensitivity to damper noise. I refer not to the groans and squeaks from missing bass-end dampers, but to the various sizzling noises which indicate some missing dampers near the treble end. Luckily this slight noise goes unnoticed by many listeners. Indeed, listening for damper noises can become a malaise affecting conscientious damper-fitters; it is far less rewarding than listening for the subtleties of the music. Then again this slight sizzling noise is masked if the music is heavy or full of decoration or accompanied by bells or other distractions. And of course there is the overriding fact that no tooth needs a damper if the intervals between its soundings are all greater than the life of its vibrations.

All these factors must have been weighed to some extent by the makers, when they decided at what point along the comb they would stop fitting pinned steel dampers. Perhaps the decision was partly forced upon them by the point at which the damper pin holes were ground away towards the lighter, treble teeth. This point varied a lot on apparently similar movements—to take for example two 13 inch 8-air Nicoles, No. 40200 has 66 pinned dampers, No. 45888 has 72.

So, then the problem arose, what to do about damping these borderline teeth? The easy answer was to continue with feather dampers, used since the early days of the industry; but I have not yet found any material adequate for this duty on these comparatively heavy teeth. A really tough plastic material does not damp them and an adequately resilient material, natural or synthetic, wears out very quickly. So the more caring makers fit-

141

ted a number of soldered steel dampers to extend the range of the pinned dampers. For example, some 8-air Conchon combs with 78 teeth had 10 soldered dampers—though this number could have been reduced if more care had been taken to preserve adequate anvils. In contrast, neither of the Nicole boxes mentioned above had any soldered dampers.

There is no doubt that all soldered dampers requiring renewal should be replaced by resoldering; but how about those combs where several teeth beyond the last pinned damper carry diminishing traces of the anvils but no steel dampers? Well, such teeth are generally too heavy (or stiff) for feather dampers and should certainly be fitted with soldered dampers, even if not previously so fitted,—unless their "damper noise" is masked by one of the factors referred to above.

So on both counts one needs to be adept at soldering dampers; and note! once mastered, it is almost as quick and just as easy as replacing pinned dampers . . . in fact quicker and easier where damper pins have to be drilled out or altered to preserve pitch.

The only additional tools needed for soldered dampers are a soldering iron, a penknife with a small blade, and a sharpening stone. The stone is merely to keep the knife blade tip truly sharp, for scraping lacquered damper wire and for cleaning and paring solder. It is very important that the soldering iron should be small—not more than 15 watts and with the tip of the bit about 1½mm dia (0.06″). You may have to file down a bit to this size; if so it must then be retinned.

Preparing the Wire

Tinned damper wire can be soldered "as is" after cleaning away any grease, but lacquered wire must have the lacquer scraped off for about 2mm, (0.1 inch) at the most. With the prepared wire, the hot soldering iron on a stand with a tiny blob of free solder on the bit, and one drop of Bakers fluid on a clean saucer, it is only necessary to dab the wire end into the fluid and then into the hot solder when it should tin the prepared 2mm. If not properly tinned, repeat. Though Bakers fluid is very undesirable on account of being so corrosive, I have found its use advisable in the minute quantity needed. Most other damper soldering is easily and better done with any good noncorrosive soldering flux.

Resoldering

Where there has already been a soldered damper, I proceed as follows:

142

1. Mark the tooth and an adjacent tooth of the same pitch.
2. Remove any remnants of old dampers with a pin after touching the old solder with the iron to melt it.
3. Scrape the old solder clean and apply a touch of flux.
4. Melt enough solder on the bit to suit the job.
5. Hold tip of prepared damper wire over the old solder and in line with tooth tip, and briefly apply iron, making sure that the wire is well below the surface of the new blob of solder. Hold steady till solder freezes.
6. Test strength of bond by lifting wire, if OK cut to length.
7. Retune to match the adjacent marked tooth by scraping away excess solder.

The amount of solder in step 4 should be enough to ensure lowering the pitch of the tooth so that it can be restored by scraping away surplus. This scraping away permits fine tuning. For step 5 it takes a bit of practice to ensure that the new wire is well below the surface of the solder, thus ensuring the bond and permitting surplus be scraped off the top. Cutting to length in step 6 depends on circumstances; if soldering onto an almost complete anvil, cut to normal length. If the anvil is entirely ground away the wire will need to be cut longer by approximately its distance below the top of a damper pin hole, say about 0.03″ (¾mm).

New Soldering

Where there has not previously been a soldered damper, two additional steps are needed:—

(a) Enough metal must be ground off the anvil remnants to compensate for the weight of solder being added. As can be seen on many a well-finished comb, this only needs an extremely small amount of solder.

(b) The ground area must then be tinned. This is sometimes difficult, and it is worth facilitating the job by initial de-greasing and by using Baker's fluid. Only a small blob of solder should be put on the bit, but after applying a spot of Bakers fluid to the tooth the bit will have to be pressed on the tooth much longer—several seconds—than for damper soldering, because the tooth must be locally heated to the temperature of the molten solder before good tinning can occur. A second small touch of Bakers fluid may be needed after the tooth area is up to temperature. Once properly tinned, as much solder as required is easily added. If that is the last use of Bakers fluid on the comb, rinse well in a solution of washing soda then hot water. Before soldering on the damper wire, check that the pitch of the tooth has been lowered; it is not easy to add solder subsequently without disturbing the wire. And be careful not to apply flux to the sides of the tooth, because if solder gets onto the sides it is a tedious job to remove it, and if not removed it spoils the appearance of the comb.

Damper Details

Occasionally a damper pin hole drilled too high on the anvil or burst open by a strong-armed redamperer necessitates a soldered damper quite a distance from the treble end, in which case it will need the same thickness of damper wire as its neighbours. Otherwise soldered dampers almost always need 0.06mm or finer wire. A common error seen in soldered dampers, particularly where there is no anvil remnant, is that they are cut too short. This means that they are too stiff and thereby likely to be ineffective. All dampers, soldered or pinned, should be of the same form throughout the comb if they are to give the appropriate damping action for a given wire thickness. This simply involves giving the extra length described above; and making certain that the solder gets no nearer to the tooth tip than the line of the anvils.

Two experts with whom I discussed soldered dampers expressed anxiety about the soldering heat annealing the damper wire, thereby reducing its springiness. But soft solder melts at 180°C which is well below the annealing temperature of spring steel; so the only danger is from using too large or too hot an iron. Hence the advice to use a 12 or 15 watt iron. I have held a 15 watt iron in contact with damper wire for many seconds without any trace of softening.

Soldering Technique

A problem faced by the amateur is that he only uses some of his craft skills spasmodically, so it is all too easy to get out of practice. This applies to such crafts as soldering, where it is easy to forget the two factors of paramount importance, namely cleanliness and matching the soldering iron to the job.

The first aspect of cleanliness is in preparing the faces to be soldered. Properly cleaned, the solder will unite with the merest trace of flux and this further ensures a top-class joint. Lavish second helpings of flux are a signal of dirty work. More subtly, the faces of the soldering bit should be flat, free from pitting or other blemishes, and properly tinned: failing these features, it will not carry out its first duty of transfering heat as rapidly as possible to the work. This rapid transfer is important, to prevent the heat spreading to other parts of the work. So, the correct condition of the soldering bit constitutes the second aspect of cleanliness—the one which is more often than not overlooked.

Matching the iron to the job is best illustrated by two examples. To affix those fiddling soldered dampers, first tin, as lightly as practicable, both the anchoring point on the tooth and the damper wire end. Then a 15-watt iron with the smallest bit is ample for touching the two tinned surfaces together and making a perfect joint. At the other end of the scale, to solder on a new lead tuning weight, after matching the surfaces and tinning, the technique is to ensure that they both quickly reach the soldering temperature. It is therefore necessary to use a large bit, with a flat edge to make maximum possible contact with the top of the tooth opposite to the lead; and if an electric iron is used, the ideal is 175 watts. Though not essential if the job is completed in a few seconds, which it should be, I always take the extra precaution of slipping a few thicknesses of dampened newspaper between the adjacent teeth.

Most restorers have seen patches of virulent red rust underneath combs. This is generally due to a lazy solderer failing to neutralize corrosive fluxes (such as Bakers fluid) which is so easily done by immersing the soldered job bodily in a strong solution of washing soda. Use it as hot as possible, rinse in equally hot water, mop off surplus and then dry it on a hot surface.

Tune Change Cam

Most cylinder musical boxes, both key wind and lever wind, have the same design of tune change lever—a piece pivoted to the bedplate, sprung to assume positive on and off positions, and carrying a curved finger to engage the tune change cam or snail. The depth of engagement is not very critical, but if it is inadequate a tune may repeat if its tooth on the cam has become slightly shortened; and excessive engagement can, where there are more than eight tunes, cause the cam to move on two teeth thereby omitting a tune.

These are the three important fixes:

1. The normal playing position of the register peg of the cylinder on the snail cam depends solely on the placing of the peg on the cylinder. (Early boxes had a wedge instead of a simple peg).

145

2. The advancing of the snail cam by one tooth for each revolution of the cylinder depends solely on the depth of engagement of the change lever finger with the tooth, as measured along a radius of the great wheel.
3. When the engagement is correct, the timing of the tune change depends solely on the height of the finger tip above the bedplate.

Now to examine these fixes in more detail . . .

1. The register peg or wedge should always be in the centre of a cam step while playing, as shown in Fig 7-7. If it is off centre there is a real danger of it coming to rest part way along the riser to the next step which causes garbling. The greater the number of tunes the shorter each cam step becomes and therefore the more important it is to ensure that the

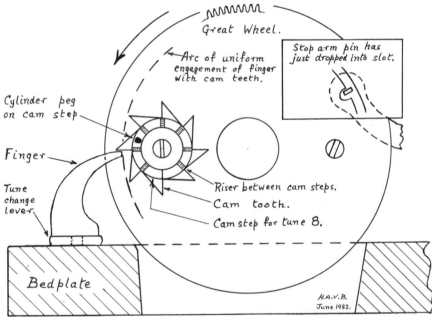

Fig 7-7 Great wheel and tune-change mechanism, viewed from the bass end with cylinder removed. Inset shows the track with stopping slot on the back face of the great wheel, and the stop arm and pin.

peg dwells near the centre of each step. This can only be corrected by adjusting the position of the peg or wedge on the cylinder.

2. If the finger on the tune change lever is set too close to the snail cam it will turn two teeth at each engagement; the correct setting is such that if set for example to pick tooth no. 2 it will just miss contact with tooth no. 3. If any tooth is then overlength it will not miss the finger and well be turned on two tunes,—a method sometimes used to delete a tune which has suffered a run. The setting of the finger must be measured radially, that is, the correct depth of engagement of the finger is measured from the periphery of the great wheel along a radius. The star wheels of a disc musical box work on exactly the same principle.

3. Having established this correct radial engagement, the next problem is so to position the finger above the bedplate that the tune change will occur at the desired period during the passage of the gap in the cylinder pins. If the finger is simply raised or lowered this will alter the radial setting and thereby upset the engagement. This particularly applies when the tip of the finger is not at the same height as the cylinder axis. Three steps are needed to modify the tune-change position without affecting the engagement . . .

(a) Mark the present position of the start of tune change on the cylinder, and then mark the preferred positon. Measure their distance apart.

(b) Mark this distance on the inside of the great wheel, starting at the present position of the tip of the finger and measuring along its arc. For meticulous accuracy these two circumferential measurements should be made at the same radii or corrected to suit.

(c) Alter the finger to meet the new position.

Step (c) may involve making a new finger, for which ordinary mild steel is adequate. Its base peg should fit closely in the square in the tune change lever and, after riveting over, should be filed and polished flush with the underside of the lever. Be sure the finger engages almost the full width of the snail cam teeth, and check that it does not run against the great wheel.

All this work should be done before cleaning the cylinder and with only the cylinder and the governor mounted on the bedplate. The governor should have the endless removed to allow free rotation of the cylinder so that it can be turned quickly to check the operation of the tune change and stop arm.

The cylinder stopping position depends solely on the point at which the trailing edge of the stop arm peg passes the leading edge of the slot in the great wheel groove,—the condition shown inset in Fig. 7-7. I doubt whether any makers had a definite policy about the cylinder stop and the tune change positions, but if they had it was certainly gone by the time they had changed from the wedge to the peg type of cam follower; the wedge with its adjustable position and clear operating line was far easier to set accurately though quite a bit more costly in material and labour.

I prefer the mechanism to stop immediately after the longest tune is finished, and the tune change to be completed just before the first note of the earliest starting tune sounded. If both of these are well timed, the mechanism has sufficient space to gather speed before it feels the drag of the peg or wedge climbing the next riser on the snail cam. This setting has the great advantage that you can choose, while the mechanism is at rest, whether to repeat or change the tune. But, it does need some finesse in setting which is probably why many boxes are set to complete the tune change soon after the end of the tune and before stopping. If they fail to complete the tune change, and the control is then moved to repeat, the next playing will be garbled.

It is not worthwhile altering the setting on a box in good condition and working nicely; but where the whole tune change mechanism needs overhaul it is an opportunity work taking.

Cylinders playing only 3 or 4 tunes have a longer period of engagement between finger and cam teeth, but the risers on the cam are exactly the same and all the foregoing theory applies. One can visualize a 4-tune snail cam from the accompanying diagram by simply omitting alternate teeth and their corresponding risers, resulting in the cam steps being slightly over twice as long and each tooth having to be turned twice as far by the finger set further in. In most boxes the height of each riser on the snail cam is $\frac{1}{60}$ of an inch, ie 0.017". Even this small distance takes some shifting against the return spring, so it is worth making sure the snail cam rotates freely and presents a smooth, burr-free face to the great wheel.

The working, radial faces of the cam teeth are generally in line with the risers, as shown in the diagram, and thus the sloping faces of the teeth coincide with the cam steps. By numbering these sloping faces it is therefore easy to see at a glance which tune is playing. Surprisingly, one very seldom finds such numbering, though it would have been a very economical gimmick so to do,—preferably on teeth slightly widened to give more space and better visibility.

148

Twelve-Tune Snail Cam

The old-established musical box makers had been in business for around fifty years before they produced movements with snail cams having more than eight steps. Earlier boxes with more than eight airs were of the two-per-turn type, and it is clear that the makers were worried by the blow on the snail from a cylinder springing back to tune 1 from say tune 12,—a distance $\frac{3}{16}$ inch, nearly 5mm. A long cylinder required quite a strong spring to make certain it returned promptly to tune 1, and a strong spring propelling a heavy weight through nearly a $\frac{1}{4}$ inch provides a hammer-blow of the steel cam follower onto thé brass cam. This, repeated hundreds of times, could gradually dig a hollow in the first cam step. Also, it could gradually force the cam follower closer to the cylinder end cap in those common cases where the early type of nonadjustable cam follower was adjusted by chisel blows on the brass behind it (a crude and unsightly practice about which every classy craftsman must have had qualms).

So when, at about the end of the key-wind era, the standard 2 inch cylinders began to appear with 10 or 12 tunes at one-per-turn, it soon became the practice to soften the blow on the cam. There were two basic methods, (1) a half-way step from last to first tune so as to take the blow in two stages, and (2) a separate stop bar fitted to the cylinder to strike the surface of the great wheel at first tune position.

Method (2) was rare, and by far the less satisfactory because if so adjusted that it prevented the cam follower from even touching the first step of the cam, then the cam was left loose and a source of stray vibrations. It probably only arose because of the two factors that made method (1) more difficult, namely that with more tunes each cam step is shortened and that with the screwed square peg type of cam follower, with its rounded corners, the point of release from the last tune step is rather indeterminate.

Method (1) came in different guises. Usually it was simply a narrow ledge in the otherwise vertical face of the drop from the last tune. This ledge was normally at the halfway point, which was the safest from the point of view of preventing it being missed by premature rotation of the snail, but less satisfactory in only saving about half the blow.

Some makers increased the snail cam diameter to give longer steps and some inserted a steel strip or peg to form the halfway ledge. Others, it has to be recorded, did nothing; and one occasionally sees 12-air boxes with the bottom step well battered. Even a 6 inch cylinder can make its mark on brass, given time.

Some makers wisely retained the old type of cam follower with sharp release edge and chamfered leading edge which could ride comfortably up an almost vertical rise to each cam step. This allowed the step faces to be longer, a decided advantage with 12-air boxes as less accuracy was needed in the position of the cam follower on the cylinder.

Another source of damage to a snail is a run, during which a peg type of cam follower can dig quite a deep groove through all the risers and the step faces.

To correct a damaged snail, first calculate the cylinder shift per tune. For accuracy measure the length of 10 cylinder track lines and divide by 10, then divide the result by the number of tunes. Answer is almost certain to be 0.017" = 0.43mm. Then clean up the lowest step of the snail cam, check each step with a micrometer and adjust with fine file as necessary.

There is a remote possibility that, due to a pricking error, one or more tune tracks may be displaced. To check this run all tunes before adjusting the cam, and note which tunes, if any, have their pins off centre of their comb teeth; any such deviations should agree with deviations in the cam step heights.

Governor

The governor, driven by the great wheel, is simply an elegantly designed air-brake. It consists of a first spindle with pinion and gear, a second spindle with pinion and wormwheel, and a vertical worm with shaft extended to carry the stop tail and adjustable air-brake which comprises two or sometimes three pivoted brass fan blades. The brake is often called the butterfly or sometimes the flyer (French: volant) and the worm is often called the endless. The thrust of the wormwheel on the worm is taken by the jewel or end-stone fixed on the governor cock. The air-brake adjustment is by moving the blades so as to sweep more or less air, and it should only be made with the worm shaft taken out of the governor because it is hard and brittle.

The only changes ever made in governor design were to replace the fixed lower worm bearing shown in Fig. 3-11 with an adjustable version controlled by a flat-headed screw immediately below the screw securing the cock, and some modifications to the air-brake. Larger movements of-

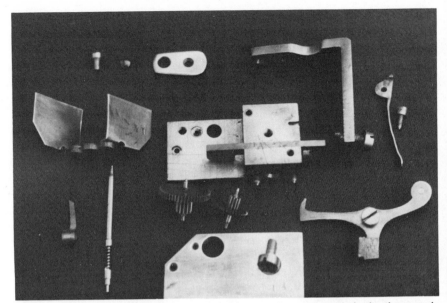

Fig 7-8 The components of a governor. These parts were made in the thousands and supplied to most makers so they give no clue to the maker of a musical box unless they are identified by a stamp on the governor cock or, occasionally, on the body. Even then, a different governor or part may have been substituted during a repair!

ten had three fan blades; and on organ boxes, where the first gear shaft took the reciprocating load of the bellows, the blades were spring-loaded so as to reduce their braking effort if the speed decreased. Some makers put these spring-loaded governors (Volant compensé) on other boxes.

Governor gear ratios and the scope of air-brake adjustment are given in Chapter 1, Table 2.

Unwise tinkering with the governor while the spring is wound up can cause a 'run' in four ways: by unscrewing the whole governor; by unscrewing the cock; by unscrewing the adjustable worm bearing till the worm comes out of mesh with the wormwheel; and by breaking the worm shaft. I fear all these have happened quite often to cylinder musical boxes. A 'run' can also arise from mechanical failure, such as a gear coming loose from its pinion or a metal fault or bad repair causing a spindle to fracture; but these, from enquiries I have made, are exceedingly rare. I have no doubt that at least 95% of all 'runs' have been caused by busy, but unwise fingers. A shoulder below the top bearing prevents the endless lifting out of its lower bearing if the end-stone is removed; but there is always the chance of a replacement endless lacking this finesse so it is unwise to release the end-stone when the spring is wound up.

Governors suffer several minor and one major point of wear. The minor points are elongated bearings, wear of pinion teeth, roughening of worm thread and top of worm shaft, and spot wear on jewel. The bearings can stand considerable play before performance is affected and only then is bushing needed. The worm thread and domed shaft top polishing are simple operations and a piece of razor blade can temporarily replace a jewel.

The major point of wear, and the cause of most governor problems, is at the teeth of the wormwheel. Ideally these teeth are angled both forward and parallel to the mating worm thread, on which they have line contact. Such a wormwheel when new is not critical as to depth of mesh; but after considerable wear, when small flats can be seen at the edges of the teeth, the meshing becomes very critical. For this reason, if the teeth show distinct wear and the governor is a reluctant starter, it is wise not to dismantle or clean the wormwheel and not to move the lower bearing; simply clean the four oil sinks and reoil, remove and polish the worm and domed top and clean and reoil its bearings and replace the jewel or move it a bit sideways to present undamaged surface to the domed top of the shaft. Then on reassembly the governor should perform at least as well as before. If it does not, a very slight adjustment to the lower bearing is worth trying. If this fails a new wormwheel is needed and luckily several reliable firms now offer this service; it restores a governor to the desirable condition in which slight upward pressure on the first gear will unhesitatingly rotate the endless.

When an old governor is found in this happy state it is safe to dismantle it completely for cleaning. The six bearings should be cleaned out with pegwood after polishing to remove all traces of abrasive polish.

Speed Control

About the middle of the 1880s some makers added a speed controller over the governor cock, usually labelled *Presto* and *Andante*. *Presto* gave normal running, and turning the knob to *Andante* moved a brass finger sideways against the top shoulder of the endless, thereby slightly reducing its speed. Another version had a friction disc at the top of the endless.

Fig 7-9 Speed controller on Baker-Troll Serial No. 15546. One of the nickel-plated fan blades is reflecting the great wheelgear teeth! The pegs on the great wheel are to engage with the safety check pivoted on the cylinder bearing bracket. At the right is the tune selector.

Governor Stop Tail

Occasionally (but still too often) one sees and hears a cylinder musical box pressing gamely on despite the fact that the pin of the stop arm is scraping round the surface of the great wheel below its correct groove. This is almost always caused by the stop tail on the endless becoming loose. It then fails to stop the endless when the pin drops into its slot and so either the mechanism will be stopped by the pin binding in the slot or the pin will be dragged over the trailing edge of the slot; after which it starts machining a new groove around the great wheel, not a pretty sight.

There are two important design rules concerning the stop tail: (1) the ring is so formed that the blow on the tail when suddenly stopped tends to tighten it; and (2) the bore of the ring is tapered to suit the tapered top half of the endless.

153

The first rule is broken if the stop tail is replaced upside down—every stop then tends to loosen it by unwinding the ring. The second rule is broken if the ring has been carelessly tightened; the correct procedure is to clinch it closely around the tapered part of the endless rather higher than its running position. Squeeze the outside of the ring all round till it is a close fit on the taper. Then hold the taper above it with soft-jawed pliers and pull the ring firmly right down against its locating ring just above the worm. It should be a tight but not a binding fit, but better too tight than not tight enough. The tail normally emerges from the upper part of the ring.

Care is needed in setting the height of the tail. In its working position, lifted against the jewel, the tail should just clear the stop arm catch when the stop arm pin is riding in its groove. If so set the tail will stop immediately when the pin falls into the slot. If the tail is set too high it will bounce off the catch a few times before stopping, thereby ruining the aftersound effect. This setting is best done with only the cylinder and governor assembled on the bedplate.

Bedplate Cosmetics

Almost everyone winces to see paint sloshed on anyhow over an unprepared surface, yet I am sorry to say this is often the fate of cast iron bedplates as any auction viewing will confirm. Though it is easy enough to excuse short cuts, I will outline the only treatment I have found to give perfect results. . . .

After removing all attachments from the bedplate:

1. Wash in hot water and detergent.
2. Apply paint stripper and scrub off till only the faintest traces of gold (or silver) remain.
3. Clean out screw and dowel holes, wash in hot water and dry.
4. Use a pointed hardened tool to score along each groove in the working surface. A fairly good second best to this tedious task is to brush along the grooves with a fine wire brush.
5. Correct any damaged or raised areas around screw holes with a smooth file.
6. Dust off, then wipe over with cloth moistened in methylated spirits.
7. Apply two coats of Ardenbrite Sovereign Gold (or silver for Nickel-plated movements). It is better to avoid painting over the line of comb screw holes and dowel holes.
8. Clean out screw and dowel holes.

The difference between this treatment and the simple addition of more paint amply rewards the effort. But, when should it be done? Taking the comb off the bedplate several times for adjustment inevitably leads to some marking of the gold paint and so I advise getting the comb right before the bedplate is painted.

Main Spring

Musical box driving springs are very powerful compared with clock and gramophone springs. A typical spring for 13 inch cylinder is about 2 metres long by 30mm wide by 0.6mm thick; and this is modest compared with the springs on Grand Format and Orchestral boxes. The spring power depends mainly on its thickness which is always, and appropriately, referred to as the 'strength'.

Before doing any work on the spring it must be completely run down. First remove the comb, then the female Geneva stop, and then allow the movement to run till the endless is no longer lifted against the jewel.

The Swiss craftsmen usually marked assembly and screw positions with one or more centre dots or assembly numbers, and these should be observed when unscrewing the spring arbor bearing brackets and when dismantling the male Geneva stop and the winding ratchet from their squares—often they only fit correctly when reassembled dot-facing-dot.

There is usually a slot in the spring cover, with its mating position marked on the barrel, and by inserting a screwdriver of the same width the cover is easily levered off. If there is no slot, strike the arbor on a wood block to eject the cover.

Remove the arbor by "unscrewing" it from the spring, and examine the spring end to be sure it is free from cracks around the hole which engages the peg on the arbor. If cracked the spring must be removed from the barrel for which I advise professional help; it is a dangerous job because the free diameter of the spring is well over a foot and it flies out to this size if removed from the barrel without restraint.

The repair procedure is to cut off the cracked end and then to soften about 2 1/2 inches by heating to dull red and allowing to cool slowly. Then make a new slot for the arbor peg, with well-rounded and smoothed corners to inhibit future cracking. Finally curve the end to suit the arbor. If the spring is broken near the middle it is much easier to extract (with protective gloves) but it cannot be satisfactorily repaired: the options are to use one-half (involving much winding) or to get a new spring—professional restorers will supply and fit.

Fig 7-10   All the components of a lever-wind spring drive except the female Geneva stop and its screw. The spring has a typical coating of hardened grease and verdigris, and needs the full cleaning treatment.

If the spring is undamanged, but looks dry, or dirty with hardened grease and quite likely patches of verdigris, it should be soaked for a day in kerosene or white spirit, ideally with the coils separated. I do this by holding the Geneva square in a vice and using a rubber-faced clamp on the barrel gear to wind up the spring about three turns. Then while slowly releasing it, I put spacers between the coils to aid solvent penetration. The spacers must be of soft metal to avoid scratching the spring which could start new cracks; mine are brass, 1/32 × 1/4 × 3 inches (1 × 5 × 70mm).

Allow a few more hours in a warm place for the solvent to evaporate completely and then insert lubricant between the spring coils before winding again to extract the spacers. I think any top quality oil will serve, but a commonly advised mixture is equal parts of clock oil and graphite or molybdenum grease.

However carefully lubricated, some springs persist in giving a shudder during unwinding, caused by adjacent coils suddenly freeing themselves after clinging together. This may be due to a slight distortion in the steel strip before it was coiled. Though harmless, it is hard on sensitive listeners who get a fright when it happens in the middle of a tune.

If there was a cardboard washer between the spring and the cover this should be renewed; and the cover is sprung back into its marked position by placing the barrel on a wood block with hole to clear the arbor and then hammering a hardwood block placed over the cover.

Some makers used stronger springs to allow smaller cylinder drive gears hence longer playing for less winding; but the preferred method was to use double or occasionally quadruple springs, generally arranged in co-axial pairs.

Double Springs

Luckily double-spring drives seem less prone to spring defects, perhaps because they are mainly on later boxes and because the strains imposed by ham-handed winders are spread over the two springs. If they have to be taken apart pay rigorous attention to marking all components and reassembling correctly because they are not interchangeable. The two covers are between the two cores on the shared arbor; if they have to be removed one core can be freed by punching out the steel hook. To reassemble the covers, thin clamps or wedges are needed as they are very close together. When correctly reassembled the Geneva stops keep in step throughout winding and unwinding.

Snug Fit In Case

Far too many cylinder musical movements are incorrectly fitted in their cases, causing a loss of sound volume and quality, particularly in the bass range.

The criteria for correct fitting of those movements which are secured by two or occasionally three screws at front and back are . . .

1. All three or four bedplate legs resting firmly on the bottom of the case which is the soundboard.
2. Gaps between the bedplate securing pad faces and the case wood-work closed completely by spacers.
3. Securing screws turning freely in their case holes throughout tighten-ing.

Why are these three easy criteria so often not met? Mainly I think on account of damage gradually caused by screws working loose and thereafter being tightened without spacers in position. Lever winding puts more strain on the bass end back screw than key winding, and the strain is considerable when the spring is extra powerful as with "fat cylinder" and organ boxes.

Early boxes were made with the woodwork a snug fit to the bedplate, but later it was found easier and cheaper to allow a tolerance of a millimetre or two and to wedge spacers into the gaps before screwing up. If the screws worked loose and/or spacers got lost, this and other ill-treatment led to the bedplate legs hammering the case bottom and could even result in bent case screws,—the bending generally occurring at the end of the threaded portion.

It is no good adjusting the bedplate legs on a nice flat table; they must be adjusted to suit their actual working positions on the bottom of the case, and so adjusted that the tapped holes in the bedplate are well centred in the case holes.

Having achieved this and straightened any bent screws, it is only necessary to insert push-fit spacers straddling the case screws. This is to ensure that when the screws are well tightened they will not cause more than a minimal deflection of the front or back of the case.

Bells in View

I have found that almost everyone, irrespective of age, sex, or qualifications, enjoys bell boxes—particularly those with bells in view. Seeing the bells being struck, specially with exotic strikers, has more general appeal than the extra subtleties of the earlier, hidden bell boxes. When correctly set up the bells pick out key notes very pleasantly, and with attractive precision; and in a well arranged box it is interesting to compare the tunes with and without the bells. The better 3-bell boxes, generally those with not more than eight tunes, are far from negligible in this respect but it does seem to be accepted that the ideal is the 6-bell or 9-bell box.

There are not necessarily as many bell teeth on the comb as there are bells. I have seen many boxes with two bells operated from one tooth perhaps with the intention of exploiting one potentially louder strike, or possibly to add an extra bell for appearances' sake. I have seen a Bremond 10-bell box with the two top treble bells worked from one tooth, and a Baker Troll 10-bell with two linked bells in the middle range, both boxes having only nine teeth in ther bell combs. An extension of this principle is

158

not uncommon in 9-bell boxes with only six bell teeth, rather disconcerting because the nine bells produce only six bell notes. I have not yet heard such a box performing any better than a straightforward 6-bell box. Strangely, the paired bells seem to sound no louder than the singles.

It is extremely rare to hear a properly adjusted bell box at an auction viewing. The cylinder pins for the bells are very vulnerable, I think because busy fingers have at some time interfered with the bell strikers. Also the strikers are often badly out of adjustment or even broken and, strange but true, the bells are quite often assembled in the wrong order. The net result of these very common faults is that restoration of a bell box can be exceptionally rewarding.

Restoration

It is doubly important to note down all damaged items and irregularities in performance before stripping, and I always make a rough diagram showing which comb tooth operates which bell because it is very easy to get muddled; sometimes the bell rods are not numbered to aid reassembly; and where the bells are mounted in a symmetrical pattern (as opposed to mounting in order of pitch) there is no relationship between tooth position and bell position. So during stripping all bells and bell components should be checked for clear marking. It is also worth checking that the bells are in their correct positions; luckily they were always pinned in pitch order so if you lift and release the bell teeth progressively from base to treble the pitch of the bells struck should get progressively higher. Having to dismantle again to correct an error is particularly aggravating with bell boxes, hence all these precautions.

I must say I prefer working on a box with a separate comb for the bells, but it is in no way detrimental to quality if the bells are operated from teeth at or near the bass end of the music comb. Many top quality boxes by Bremond, Heller and Ducommon-Girod were made in this way.

General Procedure

Whether or not the combs are integral there are the same three essential steps before doing any work on setting up the bells. . . .

1. Disconnct the bell links from the comb teeth.
2. Complete any necessary work on the cylinder.
3. Complete any necessary work on the comb operating the bells and

159

Fig 7-11 Underside of drum-and-bell mechanism Serial No. 12621. The combined, felt-padded stop plate held by two screws is in position, but the On/Off lever for the bells has been removed to show the connecting pivots between the brass bars under the comb teeth and the links to the nine bell rods.

then set it up so that the lift of the teeth is correct and the bell teeth brass bars all fall back firmly onto their felt pad. The lift should be the same as the bass music teeth. The typical mechanism is shown in Fig. 7-11.

Detail Procedure

The trickiest extra job with bell boxes is the removing and later replacing of the small headless brass pins connecting the links to the brass bars soldered under the comb teeth. For these two operations the movement must be firmly supported upside down, using a thick block under each end of the bedplate. One by one each brass bar is pulled back just far enough to bring its pin clear of its neighbours, and the pin is pushed out and stored in sequence for reuse. The pins are about 1/16 inch diameter (1 1/2mm) by the same length as the thickness of the brass bar. Extraction is facilitated

160

by using a piece of steel wire about 1mm diameter with a very short length one end bent to a sharp right angle which can then be squeezed against one end of the pin. These pins are held in position simply by being a gentle interference fit in the brass bars.

It is seldom necessary to disconnect the links from the cranks on the bell striker rods, but it is important to have their flattened ends in line and to remove any bends or kinks—except in rare cases where a link is shaped to avoid a foul. It is strange how often these simple straight links look really battered. Check also that the slits in the brass bars are as narrow as possible without binding on the links; if these slits are spread open they can foul their neighbours, particularly on a 6-air movement. There is usually a lining-up hole drilled near the centre of each brass; using this and side packing and a large soldering iron it is not difficult to resolder a detached brass.

Most bells are a loose fit on an iron rod, with a coil spring one side and a knurled nut the other. It is important to have a felt washer each side of the bell and it is a desirable extra precaution against tinniness or jangling to insulate the bore of the bell from its rod with a wrap of paper or, as was done on some boxes, a winding of cotton thread.

I make the resetting of the bells the very last job in a restoration, and another advantage of the separate comb is that it can be done without the distraction of the music playing at the same time. It is not difficult to bend the striker wires till the ideal setting is reached, but it helps to use a tool like typewriter mechanics use, wide-jawed pliers with one jaw reduced to a central line and the other scooped out at the centre. Sometimes the striker wires move in grooves cut in thin wooden coverplates; check that they are still central in their grooves. Occasionally part of the bell gantry anchorage is attached to the case, instead of being exclusively supported from the bedplate; if so make sure, before setting the strikers, that the bell positions will not be altered when fixed in the case. The strikers should rest between 1mm and 2mm from their bells, and if pushed against the bell should firmly return to that gap. This firm location is due to the brass bars being very slightly sprung against the felt pad, against which all must rest. If any have been upset, for example by inaccurate resoldering, their straight line against the felt must be restored by filing or by building up—far easier to do on a separate comb!

Finally, make sure the disengaging lever is so set that it cannot pull the strikers back far enough to touch the cylinder, and that it can be released sweetly so that the bells are not subjected to an excessive rain of blows.

I have not yet come across a bell that was either out of tune or failed to ring sweetly. But sometimes a bell, though ringing sweetly enough, emits a metallic 'clonk' when struck. There are several possible causes of this sometimes baffling phenomenon—the bell being struck too far from the rim: incorrect gap between bell and striker; metallic contact between bell and support; or loose striker. The last is strange but true, and may explain why one sometimes finds the strikers soldered as well as screwed to their rods.

The bell mechanism sometimes settles a bit after overhaul and so the striker set-up should be readjusted if necessary after a few dozen playings.

Zither

When restoring a zither, the remaining tissue paper may indicate the span of teeth to cover, which almost always excluded the extreme bass and treble teeth. I think it is worth the trouble of making a cardboard comb to try the effect: take a piece of thin card about three-quarters of the comb length and two inches wide and with one straight edge, and make a dot on this edge for each tooth tip. Draw a line parallel to and half an inch away from the marked edge and cut out a series of Vs between the dots, which will leave you with a series of pointed teeth corresponding with the comb teeth. Then set the box playing and apply the cardboard comb lightly to the centres of the middle range of teeth, when the zither effect will clearly be heard. By moving the card along the comb one can decide the best span for the zither. By moving the card further from the tooth tips and altering the pressure you apply to it, the range of the zither effect can be explored.

Experts agree that ideally the tissue roll should touch the comb teeth about two-thirds of their lengths from the tips, which is why zithers are often seen not to be parallel to the cylinder. But, the large slots usually found in the fixing bracket suggests that this was a very empirical matter, and perhaps appearance was taken into account.

There is often a tendency to exaggerate or amplify musical effects, and I think some of the dislike of zithers may be due to their being set to bear too heavily on the comb teeth. When the tissue roll is applied, it should only just be deflected when it touches the comb. Sometimes it takes a rather tedious adjusting session to achieve this. And, of course, when you've done it a lot of people will still say they don't like it. . .

Unknown Maker

Boxes of unknown make almost always conform rigidly to the conventional designs, which now helps restorers and then helped the numerous parts makers. But unfortunately they occasionally succumb to somebody's bright idea. Instead of the cylinder driving gear sliding on to a square on the arbor it is screwed on, using a left-hand thread to keep it hard up against a shoulder. I suppose it may have been slightly cheaper to make, avoiding the square and the fitting of pin, whereas the internal and external threads were all done on the lathe. The end result is apt to be hard on a restorer because after a hundred years of being tightened up every time the box played, and with rusting along these two closely-mating wrought iron threads, they are extremely difficult to unscrew. The operation is not helped by the cylinder and the return spring being in the way. I tried a 24-hour soaking in penetrating oil; then some local heating; and finally a special tool engaging two holes drilled axially into the gear, before I persuaded the two to part. Of course, reassembly is nice and easy.

Buzzing Noises

Allied with restoration is the perennial problem of stray vibrations which superimpose a vague but often persistent buzzing sound on the music.

I think all makers of key-wound musical boxes added a short length of string binding around the three control levers, near the bass edge of the bedplate and sometimes also at another point of contact. Often they are in tatty condition and once I omitted to replace them, thinking they were superfluous as the levers were so strongly sprung against the bedplate, and the box suffered no resulting ill effects. But, recently I was baffled by an outbreak of persistent buzzing in a "fat cylinder" box and was surprised when I finally tracked it down to the tune change lever. A small wad of paper pushed in between it and the bedplate replaced the missing binding and brought an immediate temporary cure. So I shall have to replace the binding; and I shall not omit it again.

Another refinement, often omitted, that can result in a baffling *occasional* buzzing is the circular wire spring in the groove of the female part of the geneva stopwork. Due to wear at the main spring housing bearing this component gradually loses its snug fit to the male part, and it is also left free for a short period at each sector change. It may also have long lost its original drop of oil which would deter vibrations. It thus becomes a loose part capable of buzzing unless prevented by being sprung against the spring housing by this simple, circular wire spring with its centre or ends raised to be well proud of its groove. A new spring is easily fashioned by wrapping a piece of wire round a rod slightly smaller in diameter than the groove. Any spring steel wire of about small safety pin size will serve, preferably first softened, then bent to shape, then hardened and tempered; but, if you are in a real hurry most safety pins will stand fashioning to shape without softening and will retain adequate springiness for this simple but occasionally important job. The makers did not cut the groove merely for pleasure.

Bluing

When steel is heated, oxide films of various colours appear on the surface as the temperature increases, and they include straw colours at about 475°F (250°C) and bright blue at 570°F (300°C). These colours are a useful technical aid in tempering hardened steel as for comb teeth; but the oxide layer also reduces the liability of the steel to rusting. For this reason, coupled with the attractive appearance, it has long been common horological practice to "blue" screws and other small components. In musical boxes this bluing is uncommon with one notable exception—early cases often had the lid hinge screws blued.

The passage of time and ill-chosen screwdrivers have usually wrought havoc, but this can be repaired as follows:—

1. Clean up and polish the screw head and if necessary recut the saw slot.
2. Degrease thoroughly.
3. Heat slowly till the royal blue colour appears.
4. Quench immediately in oil.

Item 3 is best done by indirect heat, loading the screws into suitable holes drilled in a piece of sheet brass, and heating the brass adjacent to the holes.

The same indirect heating process is used for other components, such as tune indicator pointers.

If the blue colour is weak, repolish and repeat. If the blue looks mottled, it means there was some residual oil or grease, perhaps lurking in a saw slot which should be cleaned with a whittled toothpick.

164

Blued screws in polished brass hinges look grand—just like they did when the case was new in, say, 1840. They are a sign of elegance in case restoration.

Brass Springs

On small musical movements, as in photograph albums and snuff boxes, the automatic stop is usually actuated by a brass coil spring, one end hooked into the flyer bearing bracket and the other end hooked over the tail of the stop lever. These springs seem particularly vulnerable to heavy-handed adjusters, and one finds them with a straggling and debauched aspect and doing scant duty, if any.

There are three steps in the rescue operation:

1. Choose a short piece of straight wire, such as from a paperclip, which is an easy fit into the spring coils, and wind them up round it, tight and close. This is easy to do, using fine pliers.
2. Shape the two ends, again with the fine pliers, one to slip snugly over the stop lever tail and the other to hook into the hole usually provided in the flyer bracket or, failing this, to be anchored under the bracket securing screw in which case fit a brass washer between screw head and spring end.
3. Adjust the spring by bunching or stretching its coils, until it is just strong enough to make the stop lever peg snap decisively into the hole in the great wheel.

A possible cause of these little springs becoming wrecks is faulty setting of the on-off button which is usually mounted on the front of the box and whose travel is fixed by the length of the slot through which it is screwed into the slider which in turn moves the stop lever tail. This slider should be bent until when it is in the "on" (that is when it is in the playing position) the stop lever peg is held just clear of the great wheel. Then, in the "off" position, the slider will usually be up to a sixteenth of an inch clear of the tail. This setting prevents it from pulling the stop lever too far and thus gradually weakening the spring. As on large boxes, its own friction is meant to hold it firmly in either the on or the off position, and this firmness also prevents rattle.

165

Restoration Comedy

At an auction viewing in 1985 I was looking at a very well restored Nicole lever-wind which had been fitted with a well-written and matching replacement tune sheet. A lady seemed to be very taken by it and she asked me "Is this musical box brand new?" I said it was actually made well over a hundred years ago, and I thought its makers would have been quite pleased to hear her question. She seemed slightly put off, and I fancy she was thinking "but does it *look* like an antique?"

8

CASE RESTORATION

I expect we have all had the occasional experience of showing off a musical box and discovering that the case, particularly the lid inlay, got more admiration than the works and music. This only applies to a case in super condition, unhappily not the general rule: so many seem to have lived through a period when they were used as make-shift steps or as supports for scratch-bottomed lumber. The result is damaged or missing inlay and stringing, and I urge everyone who is thinking about repairing it to start by repairing the stringing, which is very easy to do.

From World of Wood, Mildenhall, Suffolk SP28 7AY you can obtain a selection of boxwood stringing: that on musical boxes is most commonly about 1/32nd of an inch wide, about 3/4mm. The only tackle needed is a few pins, razor blade, fine glass paper, a nail filed down to a fine square a bit narrower than the stringing, and some Resin W woodwork adhesive.

I proceed as follows:

1. Locate all loose stringing and lift it carefully out.
2. Use pin and filed nail to clear all debris out of the groove.
3. Cut lengths of new stringing to suit.
4. Fit into grooves. This means shaving the ends for close fitting, and checking groove is deep and uniform.
5. Squeeze a blob of adhesive onto a piece of card and use a pin or small blade to apply it thoroughly but as sparingly as possible along the bottom and sides of the groove.
6. Insert stringing and push down flush.
7. Remove surplus adhesive with small piece of moist cloth.

Fig 8-1 Unusual optical illusion device on a musical box lid, here seen after several loose and missing pieces had been refixed. This illustration shows the parts before the final sanding to remove traces of surplus adhesive.

8. Cover with a nonstick surface, *eg* polythene, and apply moderate weight to hold it all flush.

If there are areas of loose veneer adjacent to the loose or missing stringing, these must first be secured. Small areas can be stuck by working the adhesive under them, using a 0.002″ feeler blade.

Working with wood is pleasant, and if you find you like these modest stringing repairs it is not a big step to replacing bits of missing inlay. All types of veneer (and tools) can be had from World of Wood, and the method is as follows . . .

1. Clean up the edges all round and the exposed base wood.
2. Make a rubbing of the void on thin paper.
3. Glue rubbing onto matching veneer, checking grain direction.
4. Cut along the outline.
5. Stick in and weight as for stringing.

It is the cutting that needs very sharp tools and patience. Helpful books on marquetry are in most libraries. The result repays the effort and I think enhances the music. After all, most people prefer a band to be smartly uniformed!

Brass Stringing

Quite a number of musical boxes have inlaid brass stringing, which was merely a posher version of the usual boxwood stringing. The brass was generally a bit less than 1mm wide and often considerably deeper than its width. Due to wood shrinking at right angles to its grain the brass stringing was often forced upwards at one of its chamfered ends and then, caught by idle finger or energetic duster, it became dislodged and sometimes lost. So, how to replace it:

The square section brass wire is readily obtainable (eg from Yorkwire Ltd of Leeds) but is seldom straight when delivered. Sometimes it can be straightened by gripping one end in a heavy vice and applying a strong pull. If this fails the brass should be softened by heating to dull red and quenching in water, and the pull applied again.

Then cut to length and chamfer the ends to match the mating pieces of stringing. Clean out the groove very carefully and in the usual case of it being too deep, pack uniformly till the new piece of stringing fits snugly and is just level with the surface of the surrounding veneer. Remove any grease from the brass by washing with detergent, and dry thoroughly.

Any modern clear general-purpose adhesive will serve if the new stringing will lie perfectly flat in its groove; but often this is hard to achieve, and with curved stringing even harder, so holding in place by hand is the only way and then the best adhesive to use is Araldite Rapid epoxy resin. With this adhesive it it very important to be sure the room temperature is at least 60°F = 16°C, and to mix small but equal quantities of the adhesive and the hardener, and to practice the skill of quickly laying, from pin point, a small amount of the mixed adhesive uniformly along the narrow groove. It only remains workable for just over 5 minutes. Then insert the piece of stringing, carefully press down till level throughout, remove surplus adhesive and hold steadily in position: it only has to be held for another 5 minutes or so before the adhesive sets enough to hold it. You can check that it is sufficiently set by reference to the mixed adhesive left over.

A Problem With Glue

All work with adhesives presents the problem of how to hold it in position without sticking to it. The answer is now simple,—interpose pieces of the coated paper used as backing for selfadhesive labels such as car park tickets. Easily available and absolutely free.

Shrinkage

I recently measured the lid shrinkage of an 1850 musical box, which can be done when the side beading is intact, and found it to be just over a tenth of an inch on a lid 8 inches wide—a shrinkage of about 1¼%.

Normally one only notices this shrinkage on lids because it prevents the lock closing and it causes the front and back beadings on old style lids to be pushed outwards. But, of course all wood shrinks across the grain and so all musical boxes also lose height; a typical early key-wind box 3¾ inch high would shrink about 3/64 inch = 1¼ mm. This explains why sometimes on early boxes one sees the underside of the lid scored by the gear teeth on the spring barrel. These early cases were a very close fit to the mechanism and the shrinkage has brought the lid into contact.

It is now at least 80 years too late to take any remedial action, but if the lid is still touching the gear it is easy enough to file "a whisker" off the mechanism legs.

The same shrinkage phenomenon shows up with deep cases whose marquetry includes robust vertical stringing on front and sides; pieces are often found to be bowed, and have to be reduced in length before they can be replaced.

Lid Hinges

Cylinder musical box lids were normally designed to remain open at a sufficient angle to support the glass lid without danger of it slamming shut. This was easily achieved by so placing the hinges that the back overhang of the lid rested appropriately against the back of the case. A problem posed by this design feature was how to guard against the ham-fisted operator who would pick up the box by the open lid, and roughly at that. The answer was to use small screws so that they would loosen or pull out rather than split the wood. Accordingly, well fitted countersunk steel wood-screws three-eighths of an inch long and size number 3 or 4 are normally ideal. Yet I have seen inch long screws into the case, and screw points actually penetrating the lid veneer. We have all seen resulting splintered lids and case backs. One also sees hinge screws at a drunken angle, forced in anyhow over the broken-off stub of an earlier screw.

If oversize screws have been used, or if the holes are otherwise damaged, they should be plugged with wood carefully whittled to a nice fit and then pressed firmly in after coating thinly with a wood adhesive.

To remove the remnant of a broken screw. . .

1. Drill a ring of holes all round it, about half an inch deep, with a 3/64 inch (no. 56) drill.
2. Pick out the remnant.
3. Drill 1/4 inch diameter by 5/8 inch deep to clean out.
4. Procure or whittle a piece of 1/4 inch dowel, make sure it is a good fit in the hole, and press gently in after cutting to length and coating with wood adhesive.
5. Leave to dry for a couple of hours before drilling to take new screw.

With the passage of time, even the best seasoned wood shrinks slightly across but not along the grain. This is why the front beading is often pushed awry at the corners of early type lids. It is also the reason why lids often fail to shut properly, the striker plate having become perhaps a sixteenth of an inch short of the hole in the lock plate. I have known misguided people seek to remedy this by altering the hinge position on the lid, thereby causing the lid to open too far and greatly increasing the stress on the hinges. Others ruthlessly remove the striker plate peg, often in a manner frightfully reminiscent of those Wild West dentists. The correct cure is to move the striker plate forward and fill in the resulting narrow gap in the lid behind it with a matching strip of veneer.

Lid Stays

The great majority of music box lid stays were made from brass strip about one twentieth of an inch thick, both limbs being about 4 inches long between pivots and the lower limb having its lower hole slotted so as to make it easy to avoid binding in the closed position. The two limbs varied in width from about 5/16 to 5/8 inch and varied in design from quite plain to such embellishments as lyres.

Neatly fitted stays have their case anchorage just above the wooden platform of the control levers; but stays are also often found with this anchorage below the platform and a corresponding section of the wood cut away. Sometimes crude cutting proclaims later fitment, but there is no sound reason for so fitting, except in the rare case of stays without slotted holes though there is a minor advantage that the control lever assembly can be removed from the case without the fatigue of undoing the anchorage screw.

Bell boxes, and others with large lids, which have suffered a series of ill-advised adjustments to their hinges, are the most likely to need stays. Luckily they are easy to make, drilling and filing the two brass strips as a pair and using brass wire about 1/8 inch diameter for the two pin joints. Rivet them lightly, for free movement without rattle. A traditionally-shaped L-piece secures the top limb to the lid and a round-head brass screw should be used for the case anchorage, with a fibre or leather washer each side of the stay to prevent rattle. Modern bought stays are crudely finished and look terrible on a musical box, mainly due to wrong shape and excessive thickness.

In fitting the stay, be sure that the case anchorage is about a quarter of an inch nearer to the lid hinge pin than the lid anchorage so that when the lid is shut the anchorage screw will lie near the centre of the slot. Also make sure that the lid anchorage is between 1/4 to 1/2 inch to the left of the inside of the case, partly to prevent it from fouling the case anchorage and partly to apply a slight sideways tension to the stay as a further precaution against looseness and consequent rattling.

The provision of an effective lid stay is one certain way of preventing further damage to an incorrectly-hinged musical box lid. Ideally one should restore the lid to its original hinge setting, but this may be impracticable when there have been previous repairs and undesirable where the lid is heavy and so was always a borderline case for a stay. Though one is loth to add a new feature foreign to the original antique, doing so in these cases is the lesser of two evils.

But it must be done neatly. No black tape sketchily secured with drawing pins, nor knotted string and bent hooks. Where the lid is too small to warrant the usual folding brass stay, the neatest method I have seen uses two 1/2 inch no. 2 round-head brass screws with brass washers and a few inches of white woven cord, about an eighth of an inch in diameter as sold for curtain pulls.

Fit the screws first; one inside the right side of the case at its centre and 1/2 inch from the top, and the other on the horizontal centreline of the lid and about 1½ inches in from the right side, making sure it is to the right and clear of the control lever partition in a lever-wound box. Then prop the lid open at the correct angle, measure the lightly-stretched cord length between the two screw holes, and cut the cord half an inch longer. Treat both ends with woodworking or carpet adhesive, sealing all the cut fibres together, and leave to dry.

About 1/4 inch from each end pierce the cord centrally and insert the screws with their washers, polish them beforehand and screw gently home. If on closing the lid the cord fouls the case side, slacken the lid screw and rotate the cord around it till it carries enough twist always to fold just clear to the left as the lid is closed.

Tune Sheet Troubles

Tune sheets were the great silent sufferers of cylinder musical boxes. Instruction leaflets were stuffed behind them; fidgetty fingers jabbed them pointing to the tunes; sundry scribblers sometimes disfigured them; energetic dusters probably flicked them; oil somehow got on them; and their pins corroded messily. No wonder they became loose and slid around, only to be transfixed by the peg of the lock plate and then finally freed by friction with the glass lid. When at last they became detached why did no one ever slide the sad but still useful remains under the mechanism? One *never* so finds them. If loose, apparently always lost.

Refixing them seems to have been beyond the powers of early owners; and of later refixers I must say my heart sinks when I see that a generous helping of Sellotape has been applied. Why? Because in a few years, when it has aged and dirtied along the edges, someone will be horrified at the effect and will peel it off again, and in so doing will neatly remove all the writing and printing it covered, — leaving an admittedly clean but absolutely bare track.

Surprisingly few people seem to be aware that this disaster can be averted by soaking the relevant parts of the tune sheet in surgical spirit (as used similarly for removing traces of stickers from car windows). Allow a few minutes for the adhesive on the Sellotape to dissolve—the spirit can only get to it from the back—and then very gently peel off the tape. If done carefully the tune sheet surface will be practically unaffected, though if the tape has been on for a long time a track of dirt along each side may need a bit of gentle scraping or rubbing.

Tune Sheet Repair

Many tune sheets were printed in black and had an approximately symmetrical border design. So when repairs are needed, due to a corner or side having been torn off, it is helpful to make a photo copy and then to use the most similar part of the copy as a patch for the missing piece. Any unwanted detail on the part to be used can be "whited out" with white paper over the original before the copy is made.

After fitting the patch carefully to the original and gluing both onto a good card base for their future protection, two further touchings-up are needed: Indian ink applied with a fine nib to all lines broken at the join, and a water-colour wash to blend the stark white copy with the soiled, yellowed original tune sheet.

Glass Lid Lifter

A common and deplorable cosmetic deficiency in cylinder musical boxes is the glass lid lifter. Only too often one sees tattered textile remnants, or bits of string or tape or, even worse, nothing at all so that lid lifting involves finger nails. I have even seen a car key used as a brutal lever, further wrecking the thin wooden frame.

All that is needed to restore the pristine lifter is a visit to any haberdasher and the purchase of 10cm (the minimum length sold!) of nylon velvet ribbon about 1.0 inch wide (20mm or 25mm). For small boxes and where two lifters are fitted, 1/2 inch wide is appropriate. These modern ribbons are almost indistinguishable from the original velvet lifters, and one can match the colour. On Nicole and some other boxes it was somewhere between lilac and magenta. Bright red was often used on cases with black interiors. Sometimes an unfaded trace of the original colour can be found under the domed head of the original securing pin.

Cut a length of about 3 1/2 inches, such that when folded double and secured under the lid frame it protrudes about 3/4 inch for gripping and the cut ends do not show through the glass. It helps, and prevents fraying, to stick the cut ends together with a touch of Resin woodworking adhesive. After the adhesive has set, trim the jointed end and secure with two good quality drawing pins—brass or nickel to match the cylinder. Do not be tempted to improve on the original position of the lifter by placing it at the middle, or it will probably get pierced by the peg of the lock striker plate on the main lid. Then next time the lid is opened the peg will try to haul the lifter to its own level, with damaging results.

Glass Lids

Most early glass lids had their glass secured with putty or cement and this was proved to be wise, because the later lids, with glass secured by wood beading, can cause a lot of trouble and annoyance.

What happens is that the music is impaired periodically by a vibration which stops if you put a finger on the glass. This indicates that the glass is the culprit so you search for looseness and duly find a gap between glass and beading. To insert a piece of card as a convenient wedge is but the work of a moment; and success! the vibration ceases. But, before cheering, try another tune, and at some chord the dreaded vibration will start again. This is because by altering the securing point of the glass you have altered its natural frequency of vibration.

I think I am right in saying that you can only be sure of getting this natural frequency outside the danger range by making the glass integral with its wood frame; and I have certainly found that the only certain cure for persistent glass vibration is to remove and refix all the wood beading, using new fine panel pins in new positions and making sure the glass lies snugly in the rebate in the wooden frame.

I think Nicole and Conchon and some others wisely persisted with cemented glass lids right to the end; and to repair these, and to replace really recalcitrant wood beadings, I have found "Tetrion" all-purpose filler very satisfactory. It is easy to use after rehearsing on an old bit of wood and glass, and it pays to use a very stiff mixture, slightly less water than suggested in the instructions when mixing the powder. When dry it is easy to paint or stain to match the colour of the glass lid frame. Do not use ordinary glazier's putty because the linseed oil in it will not dry out in the airless confines of a music box.

175

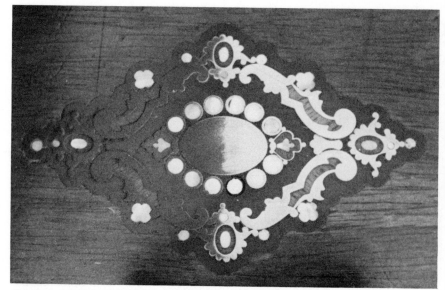

Fig 8-2 Half-cleaned brass, ebony, and mother-of-pearl inlay of fairly common type, here on Ami Rivenc/Bremond Serial No. 29290.

Patina

Dictionary definitions of patina vary widely, but generally agree that the word is derived from the Latin patina, a shallow dish, and was originally used to describe the greenish film produced by age and oxidation on bronze. The meaning was later extended to the gloss acquired with age by old wooden furniture.

Bronze, a copper/tin alloy, certainly acquires a greenish coat of oxides and carbonates, but brass, a copper/zinc alloy, goes to a very dark brown as commonly seen on the domed washers at the front and back of most cylinder musical box cases. This also occurs in varying degrees on brass inlays, and Fig. 8-2 shows an interesting example.

But stay! What causes the other type of patina, the "gloss acquired with age by old wood" so beloved by the antique furniture brigade? If you can imagine the lid of a musical box in use from say 1860 to 1900 with at least two generations of average families, it will have been dusted at least weekly and polished at least annually, but in between these attentions it

176

Fig 8-3 Delicate flower-and-leaf marquetry on domed lid of Forte Piano Serial No. 959.

will have been subject to fire and tobacco smoke, occasional dribbles of water, oil, candle-wax, accidental coughs and sneezes, dirty fingers, excreta of flies, damp bottoms of cups, mugs, and glasses. Some of these will have been wholly though more likely partly wiped or dusted off, leaving remnants to become sealed in at the next polishing. Pictures hanging on the wall are obviously less subject to these polluting influences, but even so they get absolutely masked by dirt—which one often sees being dramatically removed with cottonwool swabs by art experts on TV programmes.

When all this mess on our musical box lid has age-hardened it may well be called patina, but I must say I prefer to be without it and to see the marquetry as the case maker presented it; which is why I applaud restorers who carefully clean and lightly repolish these cases. Luckily most of the dirt has been deposited above the original french polish, and careful rubbing with 000 grade wire wool dipped in a mixture of wax polish and turpentine will generally see it off. See Fig. 8-3.

Inlay

It is a simple fact that some people are more interested in the musical box case than the music. This may be partly and understandably due to the attractive inlays usually found on the lid—sometimes displayed on a domed lid which is generally agreed to give enhanced elegance. These inlays, which include some of the finest examples of the craft of marquetry, employ all types of natural and coloured wood veneers often complemented with brightly-coloured enamels and with brass and pewter. They often have great delicacy of design, and sometimes they are both apt and witty, for example the haggis on Nicole serial No. 40200 with 13 inch cylinder playing mainly Scottish airs. (This is a key-wind box, made in about 1863, at the very end of the change-over period to lever winding).

It seems to have been a general convention in the 1840 to 1860 period that overture and other movements with large-diameter cylinders should have decorations in the corners of the case lid as well as the central motif. A typical example is shown in Fig. 8-4. This convention naturally applied to the larger Grant Format boxes which generally also boasted a formidable array of brass stringing.

Fig 8-4 Typical corner marquetry on a four-overture box Serial No. 11543, unknown make, but dated 1860 in a note by its first owner. The front right corner was badly damaged and has been quite well repaired.

Fig 8-5 Unusual hunting scene on Lecoultre Mandoline Serial No. 23132. The diamond pattern of stringing is not unusual on Lecoultre boxes.

Fig 8-6 Human figures are astonishingly rare in musical box marquetry. These dancers are on Lecoultre with hidden drum and bells, Serial No. 27740, aptly playing dance tunes.

Fig 8-7 Marquetry on the domed lid but transfer pattern on the front (where there is less wear) both supported by elaborate stringing and borders, on Serial No. 5941.

9

THE MUSIC: COMPOSERS

It is intriguing to speculate exactly how the musical box makers of the mid-1800s chose the tunes and achieved such minimal duplication and such variety. One thing is abundantly clear, namely that they banked on the appeal of tunes from the most popular current composers of opera and dance music. This explains the comparative absence of other famous composers such as Schubert (1797-1828) who wrote two operas but had them rejected as lacking dramatic appeal. There were also hymn tunes and national anthems and country tunes and some unusual tunes pinned to special order, but the great majority were operatic airs and dance tunes. That, after all, was the musical field best known to likely buyers and moreover the many boxes carrying a range of dance tunes were a domestic asset for small dances.

When it came to overtures, which represented the prestige side of the business despite being deprived of orchestra and compressed into about two minutes, today's musical experts sometimes ask why Auber was so often chosen. The answer is simple—he wrote a new opera for presentation at the Opera-Comique, Paris, practically every year from 1823 to 1861. In all about 40 operas. If you do that sort of thing you get well known. Besides, some have excellent overtures.

D'Albert

Charles Louis Napoleon d'Albert, born in Hamburg in 1809, was a French dancing-master and composer. When his father—a captain in the French army—died in 1816, his mother, who was a talented musician, took him to England and started his musical education. Later he studied the piano and composition and dancing in London and in Paris. After a spell as ballet master at Covent Garden he settled in Newcastle-on-Tyne to teach dancing and compose those dance music tunes quite often heard on musical boxes. He died in London, 1886. Some of his tunes have great staying power and are still widely recognised today, both as originals and in copied versions; notable among these is the *Bridal Polka*, *Sweetheart's Waltz* and *Edinburgh Quadrille*.

Arditi

Luigi Arditi, born in Piedmont, 1822, was an Italian violinist (he studied in Milan), conductor and composer. He wrote and conducted operas in Italy. Havana and New York, then settled in London in 1858 as Conductor to Her Majesty's Theatre. His operatic tours included Berlin, St. Petersburg, Vienna and America. He conducted the Promenade Concerts at Covent Garden from 1874 to 1877. In 1891 he conducted a London opera season which included *Cavalleria Rusticana*. He published his reminiscences in New York in 1896, under the inspired title 'My Reminiscences'. Arditi tunes heard on musical boxes include his waltzes *Il Bacio* and *La Stella*. He died on May 1, 1903, at Hove near Brighton.

Auber

Daniel Francois Esprit Auber was born at Caen in 1782 and had some success as a composer during childhood. After a spell of commercial work in London he decided to make a career in music and soon achieved success in Paris with works for cello and violin. His first two operas were publicly performed but were unsuccessful, and his first operatic success came in 1820. About that time he formed a lasting friendship with the famous (and aptly named) librettist Eugene Scribe. They found an immediate artistic *rapport* and, until his death in 1861, Scribe wrote all Auber's operas. Thereafter Auber composed only two more operas, the last appearing in 1869. He died in Paris in 1871. His two main prestige appointments were as head of the Paris Conservatoire in 1842 and musical director to Napoleon III in 1857.

Naturally enough, with his annual production at the internationally famous Opera-Comique, Auber was among the leading musical figures of the period. He was a popular, benevolent but very retiring character, the exact opposite of the extrovert conductor type. Something of an epicure, and with a ready wit in quiet company, he never conducted an orchestra nor attended performances of his operas. Asked why, he said: "If I were to attend one of my works, I would not write another note of music in my life." On four occasions he collaborated with other leading composers of the day, including Hérold, Boieldieu, Carafa and Halévy.

Auber's operas named on musical box tune sheets include *Masaniello* or *la Muette de Portici (The Dumb Girl of Portici)*, 1828; *Fra Diavolo*, 1830; *Le Dieu et la bayadère (The God and the Dancing-girl)* 1830; *Gustave III* or *La Bal masquée*, 1833; *Le Cheval de Bronze (The Bronze Horse)* 1835 with a revised version in 1857; *Le Domino Noir*, 1837; and *Les Diamants de la Couronne (The Crown Diamonds)* 1841.

Most of Auber's work was melodious and elegant in the highest tradition of French comic opera (*i.e.* opera containing spoken dialogue) and is well exemplified in the overture to *The Bronze Horse*. The main exception is the famous *Dumb Girl of Portici* which was written in the best vein of traditional grand opera and duly acclaimed; and it stepped into history at its Brussels premiere in 1830 when the audience, excited by the dramatic story about tyrannical rule, rushed into the streets and passed on the message to the crowds and so led to Belgium's freedom from Dutch rule.

Audran

Another French composer of operettas, said to have rivalled Offenbach and Lecocq in popularity during the 1880's, was Edmund Audran, 1840-1901, born in Lyons to a musical family. After his musical studies he became a composer and church organist; his early compositions included a funeral march for Meyerbeer in 1864. He went on to write several successful operettas, including . . .

Le Grand Mogol	1877
Les Noces d'Olivette	1879
La Mascotte	1880
Giliette de Narbonne	1882
La Cigale et la Fourmi	
(The Grasshopper and the ant)	1886
Miss Helyett	1890
La Poupée (The doll)	1896

Tunes from the first five are quite often seen on tune sheets of cylinder musical boxes. The most successful, *La Mascotte*, has tunes on 15½ inch Polyphon Nos. 1752 and 1920 and others, and the *Grand Mogul* and *Miss Helyett* and *La Poupée* are also represented on disc. If Miss Helyett has got onto a cylinder box she is quite likely to be nickelplated.

Balfe

Michael William Balfe, son of a dancing master, was born in Dublin, 1808. His first successes were as a violinist and singer, and a patron took him to Rome in 1825. He moved on to Milan and then Paris, where his talent was spotted by Rossini who engaged him for three years as a baritone, his successes including Figaro in *The Barber of Seville*. He continued as a singer in Italy and London where in 1838 he took the role of Papageno in the first English performance of *The Magic Flute*. Meanwhile his first English opera, *The Siege of Rochelle* was staged at Drury Lane in 1835 and ran for three months. Its overture is to be found on some cylinder musical boxes.

After a spell as manager of the Lyceum theatre he migrated to Paris and wrote two operas for the *Opera Comique*. Then he returned to London in 1843 for his major success, *The Bohemian Girl*. From 1846 to 1852 he was conductor for His Majesty's Theatre.

Balfe and his wife enjoyed artistic and social successes when they visited Berlin and St. Petersburg during the 1850s, and in 1864 Balfe turned gentleman farmer at Rowney Abbey, Hertfordshire, where he died in 1870.

He wrote twenty-nine operas, including *Falstaff* 1838, *Satanella* or *The Power of Love* 1858, *Blanche de Nevers* 1863, and a posthumous work *Il Talismano* which appeared in 1874. Tunes from these are not uncommon on musical boxes, but it was *The Bohemian Girl* that really set the tune arrangers going and one often hears excellent renderings of the arias "I dreamt that I dwelt—" and "Then you'll remember me," and of the overture. They remained very popular throughout the musical box era and appeared on numerous discs. Illustrious and other bands and singers had a go at them when the gramophone arrived and in 1936 Laurel and Hardy presented them unscathed in their film which was titled, strangely enough, *The Bohemian Girl*. All this despite Balfe being dismissed as rather trivial by some writers on opera.

184

A good statue of Balfe, holding a sheaf of music, was placed in the vestibule of the Drury Lane Theatre in 1874, where it still nonchalantly stands in the company of Kean, Garrick and Shakespeare.

Bellini

Rossini, Donizetti, and Bellini are often bracketed together by lovers of Opera because they were contemporaries and because in their operas Italian melody and singing reached a peak. It is fortunate that so many of these melodies, famous and less famous, are preserved for enjoyment on musical boxes.

Vincenzo Bellini was born at Catania, Sicily, in 1801, the son of an organist. A local nobleman admired his youthful talent and paid his expenses at the *Real Conservatorio* in Naples. Young Bellini was lucky again that his first opera, in 1825, was heard by Barbaia, the manager of La Scala, Milan and of many lesser opera houses. Barbaia commissioned Bellini to write an opera for Naples and, when in 1826 it proved a success, to write another for La Scala. This was *Il Pirata* and its enthusiastic reception made the name of the young composer. He wrote in all only ten operas, those often noted on musical boxes being:

Il Pirata	1827
La Straniera	1829
I Capuletti ed i Montecchi	1830
La Sonnambula	1831
Norma	1831
Beatrice di Tenda	1833
I Puritani de Scozia	1835

Bellini was not a pioneer; his genius was all for lyrical expression and this explains the wide popularity of Bellini tunes on musical boxes. He fell seriously ill soon after the London premiere of *I Puritani* and died in Paris in September 1835, aged 34. Though obviously liked and admired by his friends he suffered severely from an inferiority complex and from imagined persecution, as can be seen from a typical letter of his in December 1831 to a friend in Catania. . . .

"In spite of a formidable cabal against it, worked up by one powerful and one very rich person, my *Norma* astounded the public even more last night at the sec-

185

ond performance than at the first. Yesterday's official gazette at Milan had announced a complete fiasco, because at the first performance the opposing party had sat in silence while the well-intentioned applauded; and because the powerful person is in command and can order the newspaper to write whatever she likes. . . . The public is cursing the journalist, my friends are jumping for joy, and I am most satisfied, doubly pleased because I have discomfited so many of my mean and powerful enemies . . ."

It is very revealing to contrast that Bellini letter with one written the day before by Donizetti to a friend in Naples . . .

"*Norma*, which had its first performance yesterday evening at the Scala, was not understood, and was judged over-hastily by the Milanese audience. For my part I should be most delighted to have composed it, and would willingly put my name to that music. The introduction and the last *finale* of the second act are enough in themselves to establish the greatest musical reputation; and the Milanese will soon realise how foolish they were to pass premature judgment on the merits of this work . . ."

In 1837 six famous pianists including Chopin and Liszt played their own variations on Bellini's march from *I Puritani* at a charity concert. The series, later orchestrated by Liszt, came to be known as the Hexameron—a neat and lasting tribute to a famous composer.

Bergson

Michael Bergson, 1820-1898, was a Polish pianist and composer. From 1863 he was a professor at the Genève Conservatory of Music, later becoming a director. He wrote an opera *Luisa di Montfort*, 1843, and many songs and dances including *I Zingari, grand caprice hongrois* and *Un orage dans les lagunes*, recorded in Fig. 5-3.

Bishop

Henry Rowley Bishop, a Londoner, 1786-1855, had an outstanding reputation in his day and he scored two notable "firsts",—he was the first musician to be knighted (in 1842) and he was the first to employ a recurring theme-tune in his opera or more strictly musical play *Clari, or the Maid of*

186

Milan, 1823. This theme song, music by Bishop and words by the American poet John Howard Payne, was "Home Sweet Home". Bishop used it again in the overture to his opera *Home Sweet Home* in 1829 and Donizetti borrowed it for use in *Anna Bolena*, 1830. Its immense popularity, often a source of irritation to classy composers, was further heightened after 1850 when it was adopted as a star turn by Jenny Lind.

Bishop's musical output between 1806 and 1836 was tremendous, covering about 125 musical plays and operas of which fifty where wholly or partly adapted from the European successes of Mozart, Rossini, Auber & Co. Most of the adaptations debased the originals and were powerfully deplored in musical circles. Bishop's own operas or plays-with-songs are now only remembered for some outstandingly popular songs and glees including "Lo, here the gentle lark" from *The Comedy of Errors*, 1819; "Bid me discourse" from *Twelfth Night*, 1820; and "Oh well do I remember" from *Maid Marian*, 1822. "Bid me discourse" is often heard on early musical boxes, and it is rather typical of Bishop that he took these words from *Venus and Adonis* and used them in *Twelfth Night*.

"Home Sweet Home" is correctly credited to Bishop on discs, including Polyphons Nos. 1381, 2199 and 5993; and his ballad "The Mistletoe Bough" is on Polyphon No. 5779. But on cylinder box tune sheets the tune is often wrongly attributed to John Sinclair, 1791-1857, a singer at Covent Garden from 1811 who created the tenor roles in some Bishop operas and who sang for Rossini and others in Europe between 1819 and 1823. He composed a number of Scottish-style songs; but why his name should be attached to "Home Sweet Home" by so many leading makers including Nicole, Mermod, Billon-Haller and Weill & Hamburg, remains shrouded in mystery.

Georges Bizet

Some famous composers are far less frequently seen on musical box tune sheets than their fame would suggest, and a good example of these is Bizet, even allowing for the fact that his composing period came relatively late.

Bizet was born of talented musical parents in Paris, 1838, which led to his exceptionally early admission to the *Conservatoire* in 1848. Taught among others by Gounod and Halévy, whose daughter he ultimately and happily married in 1869, he progressed so well that he could have made a

187

distinguished career either as a concert pianist or as a composer. By 1860 he had been acclaimed for his one-act operas and songs. Unfortunately he had breakdowns of confidence and variations in his musical ideas, and he abandoned many projects in a half-finished state. Moving in top musical circles kept him to the fore, but his successes were minor compared with his potential and talent. He also had the exceptional misfortune that his first major work to achieve parennial popularity and acclaim, the opera *Carmen*, had a cool initial reception at its Paris premiere for the very reasons of its later popularity, namely the characters were too robust or earthy or in fact too true to life, and the music was "too Wagnerian". Bizet died in 1875, before *Carmen* established its worldwide success. He did, however, enjoy a number of successes in life; and of his few published works the following appear on musical box tune sheets . . .

Pêcheurs de perles	1863
La Jolie Fille de Perth	1867
Djamileh	1872
Carmen	1875

Naturally *Carmen* is also featured on discs, typically 15½ inch Polyphon Nos. 10215-8 and 19½ inch Nos. 5239 and 50154-5.

In addition to the operas one finds two other notable Bizet compositions, *Jeux d'enfants* (1871) and his famous incidental music to the Alphonse Daudet play, *L'Arlesienne* (1872).

It will never be possible to list all the tunes that have been recorded on musical boxes, so one can always keep hoping to hear some particular favourite. One of my hopes is the overture to *Carmen*.

Cherubini

If you ask lovers of classical music, or for that matter music libraries, about Cherubini they will extol his Church music and in particular his justly famed Requiem Mass in C. But he also wrote thirty operas, some of whose tunes and overtures grace musical boxes. So, who was he?

Luigi Cherubini, son of a Florentine musician, was born in Florence in September 1760. At age 18 he was given an allowance by the Grand Duke of Tuscany to study music in Vienna. His early operas were well received and he spent the year 1785 in London as Composer to the King. In 1788, with thirteen operas already to his credit, he took up permanent residence in Paris and joined the top echelon of composers. He was appointed to the Paris *Conservatoire de Musique* when it was founded in 1795 and became its Director in 1822; consequently he influenced almost all the leading French composers of the first half of the nineteenth century. He composed a large volume of Church music and a further seventeen operas, some in collaboration with Boieldieu and others, and some in revived classical style, successor to Gluck. The better known are

Démophon	1788
Lodoïska	1791
Medea	1797
Les Deux Journées	1800
Anacréon	1803

Medea, which was revived in 1959 for Maria Callas, is regarded at his peak achievement, and *Le Deux Journées* was the most popular; but all were overtaken in popularity by the more boisterous scores of operas by Boieldieu and Auber, which may explain why they do not figure more often on musical box tune sheets. In fact the serious and perhaps rather pompous Cherubini ticked off young Boieldieu for receiving more acclaim than his music deserved, and the rebuke was apparently accepted and further study in counterpoint pursued under Cherubini the maestro. He lived till 1842, and in 1837, aged 77, he attended the Strauss first night in Paris. I think he might have been rather annoyed at getting absolutely no mention until 1976 in the 9th edition of *Kobbé's Complete Opera Book*, which is a generally useful source and is available in most libraries. Swifter justice was done in von Westerman's *Opera Guide*, a valuable and inexpensive 580-page Sphere paperback.

What a pity the tune arrangers cannot take a bow alongside the composers! My medal would go to the arranger of the Anacréon overture for Lecoultre Freres, Geneva, about 1840. After a cool start it breaks into a positively dazzling second half which keeps most of the 158 comb teeth continually working or rather, playing.

Donizetti

Undoubtedly the most hardworking of the famous trio of Italian Opera composers in the early 1800's was Donizetti, who composed more than 70 operas compared with 10 by Bellini and 36 by Rossini.

Gaetano Donizetti, born Bergamo 1797, had an orderly life based on formal musical studies starting from childhood. He had written 33 operas by 1829, all produced in Venice or Rome or Naples, etc., but he first achieved international success with his 34th, *Anna Bolena*, in 1830. He kept up his output, with rather variable quality, and naturally it is his successes that one sees on musical box tune sheets, including in particular. . . .

L'Elisir d'Amore	1832
Lucrezia Borgia	1833
Lucia di Lammermoor	1835
La Fille du Regiment	1840
La Favorite	1840
Linda di Chamounix	1842
Don Pasquale	1843

Though critics rate Donizetti least of the above named trio, he is still very well remembered for some of the operas listed above and their engaging melodies. It is unusual for a year to go by without a Donizetti revival somewhere in the U.K. He took a hand in some of his librettos and was not worried when *Lucrezia Borgia* had to be switched to Turkish characters and settings for performance in Paris after Victor Hugo stopped the use of the original text which was based on his play.

Donizetti was a modest, amiable and helpful individual. An example of the last comes in a letter written to him by young Verdi in May 1844:

"Most esteemed Maestro, it was a welcome surprise to me to read your letter to Pedroni, in which you kindly offer to attend the rehearsal of my *Ernani*. I have no hesitation in accepting your kind suggestion with the utmost gratitude, for I am certain that my music cannot but profit greatly when Donizetti deigns to give it a thought . . ."

In a letter to the publisher Cottrau in February 1845 Donizetti wrote . . .

"You see how right I was to say Verdi had talent! He is a man with a brilliant future, as you will see . . ."

Managers at that time were very powerful and could be dangerously vague about essential support, and Donizetti could take a firm line with them as shown in a letter to the director of the Academie in Paris, in 1838 . . .

"The great masters in whose footsteps I shall be following have been aided in their success by all the resources your Theatre has to offer, and you will think it only just, Monsieur, that I should claim the same assistance for myself; otherwise the contest would be too unequal and I should be rash to undertake it . . ."

Donizetti suffered his first attack of paralysis of the brain at the end of 1845 and died, very widely mourned, in Spetember 1848.

Friedrich von Flotow

Flotow (1812-1883) came from a rich and aristocratic family in Mecklen-berg. He studied at the Paris *Conservatoire* from 1828 till 1830 and of his many operas two achieved notable successes: *Alessandro Stradella* was first performed at Hamburg in 1844 and was taken up by fifteen other Ger-man theatres within a year. The title is commonly shortened to *Stradella.* An even greater success attended the 1847 Vienna premiere of *Martha.* This opera's alternative title is "Richmond Market", which the bored Lady Harriet and her companion visit disguised as servants. Martha and Julia, with serio-comic results. Lady Harriet has a show-stopper with her song in Act II—*The Last Rose of Summer.*

Stephen Foster

American composers are not often named on musical box tune sheets, so the occasional appearance of the name Christy is doubly strange, be-cause he was not a composer.

E.P.Christy was a minstrel-troupe organiser and performer, born 1815 in Philadelphia. His main period of fame was in New York between 1846 and 1854, when he often staged premieres of songs by Stephen Foster. Christy licenced another troupe of black-faced singers to appear in Eng-land at the St James theatre in 1857 and they were so successful that "Christy's Minstrels" became the generic name for Negro minstrels in the U.K.

The composer behind these successes was Stephen Collins Foster, born Pittsburgh 1826, died New York 1864. After a string of early suc-cesses he agreed with Christy in 1850 to have exclusive first-performance rights to every new song and also agreed for Christy to name himself as composer of *Old Folks at Home* (1851). Foster wrote over two hundred songs, in two main types, "minstrelsy" and "hearth and home." Perhaps the most famous minstrelsy four were . . .

Oh Susanna	1848
Nelly Bly	1849
Camptown Races	1850
Massa's In De Cold Cold Ground	1852

And perhaps the most famous hearth-and-home four were . . .

Jeanie With The Light Brown Hair	1854
Old Dog Tray	1853
My Old Kentucky Home	1853
Come Where My Love Lies Dreaming	1855

These tunes are rare on cylinder boxes, but most of them were issued on disc.

Gounod

Charles Gounod was born in Paris, 1818, his mother a pianist and his father an artist. He entered the Paris Conservatoire under Halévy and Co. in 1836. After successes with Church music he was persuaded to compose operas in 1851 and again in 1854 but neither was a success. Then came a well-received musical version of Moliere's *Le Médecin malgré lui* in 1858 soon followed by a stupendous success with *Faust* in 1859.

Gounod wrote twelve operas, the better known listed below. Tunes from *Faust* permeate cylinder and disc musical boxes, and tunes from the others turn up from time to time. Gounod also wrote numerous masses, sacred and secular songs, and orchestral works, many held in the same high musical esteem as *Faust*. He came to England in 1870 during the Franco-Prussian war and stayed till 1874, after which his composing talent declined though he had a strong and lasting influence on English choral music. The more high-brow musical set took a dim view of his two minor but lasting popular successes, namely *The Funeral March of a Marionette* and the one he ingeniously culled from a Bach prelude, *Ave Maria* (1859). This is heard effectively on fat cylinder boxes, it is not so good when shortened to one minute.

192

These are the Gounod operas likely to be found on musical boxes. . . .

Faust	1859
Philémon et Baucis	1860
La colombe (the dove)	1860
La reine de Saba	1862
Mireille	1864
Romeo et Juliette	1867
Le tribut de Zamora	1881

Gungl

Joseph Gungl was born in Hungary in 1810 and died in Germany in 1889. The apostrophe often inserted in his name is a long-standing and much-copied error. He started work as a schoolmaster, then enlisted in the Hungarian army and became a military bandmaster. He toured the Regimental band and later his own band around Europe, and in 1849 over to America, playing mainly his own compositions including his Hungarian March, opus 1. He was appointed *Musik-direktor* to the King of Prussia in 1849 and Bandmaster to the Emperor of Austria in 1858. By 1873 he had composed about three hundred dances and marches, mostly "distinguished by charming melody and marked rhythm". They included the *Eisenbahn-Dampf* (railway-steam) galop and sets of polkas, mazurkas and quadrilles entitled *Katharinen* and *Die Elfe* or, plural, *Die Elfen*, which scarcely need translating.

Note, however, that the title does not fix the composer. Different composers in the same country, and even more so in other countries, seemed to have no inhibitions about using identical titles—though probably most often in simple ignorance. So for example both *Katharinen* and *Die Elfen* are commonly found titles. Another of the *Katharinen* is a waltz by Labitzky.

Halévy

Opera composers not so frequently seen on those garlanded tune sheet pillars include Halévy and Hérold; but in fact these two were the leading composers of French operas after Auber and Meyerbeer in the period

1820 to 1850, and their tunes are often heard on cylinder musical boxes. Though less well remembered, most of the scores of their works listed below are available in the London Music Library and many of them get booked out several times every year.

Formental Halévy, 1799-1862, came from a scholarly Jewish family and entered the Paris *Conservatoire* in 1811 under Cherubini. He was appointed Professor in 1827 with a gradually extended range of musical subjects. His pupils included Gounod, Bizet, Lecocq and Saint-Saëns. He composed 36 operas the most successful being. . . .

La Juive (Jewess)	1835
L'éclair (Lightning)	1835
Guido et Ginevra	1838
Le Drapier (Draper)	1840
La Reine de Chypre (Cyprus)	1841
Charles VI	1843
Les Mousquetaires de la Reine	1846
Le Val d'Andorre	1848
La Fée aux Roses (Rose Fairy)	1849
La Magicienne	1858

Halévy was undoubtedly overshadowed by Auber and Meyerbeer, but he is featured beside them on the facade of the Paris Opera. He also got a bit of faint praise from Wagner who described him as "frank and honest: no sly, deliberate swindler like Meyerbeer".

Hérold

Ferdinand Hérold, 1791-1833, entered the Paris Conservatoire in 1806 after good grounding from his father who was a pianist, composer, and teacher. Poor health and a chronic lack of suitable scripts hindered his progress but he scored some notable successes including his ballet *La Fille mal gardée* and the following operas . . .

Le Muletier	1823
Marie	1826
Zampa	1831
Le Pré aux Clercs (Scholars' field)	1833

Hérold died of consumption aged only 42, leaving a half-finished opera *Ludovic* which was completed successfully by Halévy in 1833.

The *Zampa* overture with its powerful ending rivalled the *William Tell* and *Bohemian Girl* overtures in popularity and is often found on pianola rolls and, rather compressed, on disc,—eg Regina No. 1444.

Jullien

A composer frequently named on tune sheets in the period 1845 to 1880 is Jullien. He wrote a vast number of dance tunes and quadrilles but is best remembered as the showman-conductor who first enlivened the London Promenade Concerts in 1840 and then conducted them with unrivalled *panache* until 1859, setting the tradition which was next rekindled by Henry Wood in 1895.

Jullien was born at Sisteron in the French Alps in 1812, while his parents and three sisters were travelling from Rome to Paris. Delayed by the birth, his father played the violin for the local Philharmonic Society, the thirty-six members of which all insisted on standing as godfather to the baby. That is why young Jullien was enriched with 36 christian names (not all different) of which the first was Louis. It was a suitable prelude to a life full of amazing incidents, true and apocryphal, both sorts well described in the *Life of Jullien* by A Carse, 1951.

After a musical childhood and service in the French Navy, Jullien was accepted as a student of the Paris Conservatoire about 1833; but he was irked by the formal part of the studies and, helped initially by Rossini, quickly became notorious as a conductor of spectacular concerts which were the talk of Paris in the period 1836-38. They included fireworks and cannon, and the noise caused brushes with the police and excellent publicity. Nor was the Jullien private life tame; a dispute about the authorship of his waltz *Rosita* led to a duel in which he came off second-best but unabashed.

Jullien first conducted in England at Drury Lane in June 1840; and by 1843 he was fully established as the maestro of the Promenade Concerts. His great success lay partly in his own personality as a flambuoyant conductor, partly in his combination of popular and high-brow music, partly in his fine orchestras with top-line performers, and not least in his own topical music: his numerous quadrilles included the *British Navy* (with four military bands), the *Great Exhibition*, the *Siege of Sebastopol*, and *Les Hugue-*

nots which had a battle and conflagration in its fifth movement and was based on Meyerbeer's opera. Jullien never minded borrowing, with acknowledgement, other composers' tunes. These musical successes, coupled with a likeable and extrovert personality and a taste for colourful sartorial effect, made Jullien very popular and very newsworthy and good material for *Punch* who, in a typical 1845 cartoon, showed him tearing his hair when Queen Victoria was rumoured to have banned the polka. His corresponding financial success was boosted by his music shop at 3 Maddox Street, where his signed sheet music figured prominently and was often advertised in *The Times*.

From July 1853 to June 1854, Jullien made a triumphal American tour, giving over 200 concerts and getting superb Press notices and earning around $15,000 per month.

On three occasions Jullien departed from his *meitier* as conductor-cum-entertainer, each time with disaster. In December 1847, he launched a season of Grand Ópera at Drury Lane, and became bankrupt in February 1848. In 1852 he produced his own opera, *Pietro il Grande*, at Covent Garden but it only ran for five performances and he lost £16,000. In 1865, the new Surrey Garden Company engaged him for five years as musical director and conductor for their grandiose project of a 10,000-seater concert hall; but after one misleadingly good season it failed, causing another severe loss to Jullien. He also suffered the loss of many of his music manuscripts in the fire which gutted the Covent Garden Theatre in March 1856. Each time he came back fighting.

Jullien's last London season ended in December 1858 and rated a farewell ode in *Punch*. After a provincial tour he returned to Paris and started planning a world tour for 1860; but he had a mental breakdown and died in March a few days after being admitted to an asylum.

His tunes found on musical boxes include *Rosita, Olga*, and many other waltzes and polkas, and parts of quadrilles such as the *Sebastopol March*. Nicole 8-air boxes dated around 1860 are found with as many as three Jullien tunes, and his name appeared in print on the scrolls of some tune sheets. His biographer A Carse regretted that this eminent man was forgotten. But is he? One hears his music, and sees his name on all these tune sheets, and he even is remembered here!

Labitzky

Josef Labitzky was born in Germany in 1802 and died in 1881. After a period as first violin in bands at Marienbad and Carlsbad he formed his own orchestra and with it toured Southern Germany. Then he took a course in composing at Munich; and he published his first waltzes in 1827. In 1835 he settled in Carlsbad as director of the town's band, taking it on tour as far afield as London and St Petersburg and growing in fame both as composer and performer of light music.

Labitzky's dances were acclaimed for their rhythm and spirit. His best waltzes included *Sirenen, Aurora and Carlsbader*, and his galops were said to rival those of Strauss.

Lecocq

Although even ten thousand musical box tune sheets would be grossly inadequate as a true statistical sample, yet no one has quarrelled with the 'Top 33 operatic tunes' listed by Lyn Wright on page 290 of the summer 1982 issue of *The Music Box*. . . . and I would not mind a small bet that results from another random 500 tune sheets would retain all the named composers and at least half the named tunes.

About the middle of the list is an 1872 light opera by Lecocq, who surely thereby merits a mention.

A.C. Lecocq was born of a poor family in Paris, June 1832. His musical talent enabled him to give piano lessons at age 16, and to enter the Paris Conservatoire in 1849 where his friends included Bizet and Saint-Saëns. Not until he was forty did he achieve success, but then his first three successes in the list below were said in Paris to establish him as 'the natural successor to Offenbach'. His last successful opera appeared in 1882, but he continued with other compositions and writing till his death in 1918. His works as listed often appear on musical box tune sheets, and for example the Grand Waltz from *Les Cent Vierges* is on Polyphon 1836.

Les Cent Vierges	1872
LaFille de Mme Angot	1872
Giroflé Girofla	1874
La petite mariée	1875
La marjolaine	1877
Le petit Duc	1878
La Carmargo	1878
Le grand Casimir	1879
Janot	1881
Le coeur et la main	1882

Lefébure

Charles Edouard Lefébure, 1843-1917 was a French composer of very popular very light music. His name is more commonly spelt Lefébvre. One critic described his and similar music as "sentimental melodies, a harmonic scheme of about three chords and the tritest modulations, with run-about passages and twiddles" and quoted as an example *Les Cloches du Monastère.* It certainly gets a share of twiddles in the piccolo notes.

Lumbye

Hans Christian Lumbye, 1810-1874, a Danish conductor and composer. From 1840 he led his own orchestra in Copenhagen and around Europe in "Concerts à la Strauss", playing his own as well as the Viennese music. His dance music includes the *Amélie* waltz and polka and the (one word!) *Champagnegalop.*

Meyerbeer

One of the small groups of famous composers of Opera in Paris in the mid 19th century, who shared the librettist Scribe with Auber and who provided many excellent musical box tunes, was Giacomo Meyerbeer (real name L Beer). Born in Berlin in 1791 to a wealthy German-Jewish business family, he achieved quite a reputation as a pianist, but soon realised he would never rank among the great and so turned to composition. His first operas, some in German and some in Italian, achieved mild success, but again he perceived that something extra was needed to achieve major success. Accordingly, he settled in Paris and, correctly sensing the current local desire for spectacle, adopted a flamboyant style, doing everything bigger and louder and sometimes better. He included spectacular ballets, and music which sometimes taxed the singers, but all based on first class librettos by the acknowledged master-hand of Eugene Scribe.

The Meyerbeer operas often noted on musical box tune sheets, with the dates of their first performances are:

Robert le Diable	1831
Les Huguenots	1836

Le Prophète	1849
L'Etoile du Nord	1854
Dinorah	1859
L'Africaine	1865

Meyerbeer's sustained success kept him high in the musical hierarchy and led to his appointment as Royal Director of Opera at Berlin and he divided his time between Berlin and Paris till his death in 1864. He spent many years perfecting his last opera. *L'Africaine*, and to conserve his energy he reused the music from one of his German operas in *Dinorah*.

The popular acclaim given to his grandiose style brought tetchy comments from Wagner and Schumann among others, who referred to him as "that Jew banker" and "like those circus people." But audiences persisted in liking these powerful effects and, for example, the enormous bell of the Paris Opera was specially cast in 1836 to sound the tocsin in Act IV of *Les Huguenots*, the signal for the start of the massacre. Several of the Meyerbeer tunes must have been associated with such effects, as they appear, well arranged, on drum and bell boxes. And they are not only heard on musical boxes today; the *March of the Huguenots*, gets good military band airings because it is an adopted slow march of the Guards, heard when Trooping the Colour.

Moving in wealthy circles, Meyerbeer must have heard many of his overtures and melodies on musical boxes and he certainly would not have hesitated to complain if he had disliked the arrangements.

Offenbach

In 1980, the centenary of Offenbach was well marked by many revivals, and books and articles by sundry experts; though I must say they failed to record his standing on musical box tune sheets. So there is a gap worth filling.

Jacques Offenbach was born Jakob Eberst in Cologne, 1819, son of the Cantor of the Synagogue. He spent an undistinguished year in the 'cello class of the Paris Conservatoire and in 1834 joined the orchestra of the Opera Comique. His first success as a composer did not come till 1855 when he became manager of a small theatre in the Champ Elysées. That same year he took over a theatre in the Passage Choiseul, renamed it Les Bouffes-Parisiens, and launched his successful series of light, satirical

Operettas; those most often noted on musical boxes are listed below with dates of first performances. Offenbach died in Paris in 1880, just too soon to see his only Opera (as opposed to Operettas) which opened in February 1881 and ran for 101 nights that year.

Orpheus in the Underworld	1858
Geneviève de Brabant	1859
Daphnis et Chloë	1860
La Belle Hélène	1864
Bluebeard	1866
La Vie Parisienne	1866
La Grand-Duchesse de Gérolstein	1867
La Périchole	1868
La Princesse de Trébizonde	1869
Madame Favart	1878
La Fille du Tambour-Major	1879
Tales of Hoffmann	1881

It is rather surprising that one does not find overture boxes playing Offenbach overtures. Perhaps they were considered too "light", and of course they only appeared at the end of the golden era of overture boxes.

Osborne

George Alexander Osborne, whose father was an organist and lay-vicar, was born at Limerick in 1806. He was self-taught until at the age of eighteen he went to Belgium and to Paris to study the piano. He gained considerable success in Paris where his friends included Chopin and Berlioz. In 1843 he settled in London and for many years ranked as an esteemed and genial teacher of the piano. He died in London in 1893. He wrote numerous piano/violin duets, and piano solos of which one achieved extraordinary popularity in the 1860s. It was very descriptively titled *La Pluie des Perles* (Rain of Pearls) and is found on musical boxes.

Emile Paladilhe

A tune often heard and enjoyed on cylinder musical boxes is *Mandolinata*—and not surprisingly it is particularly to be noted on the tune sheets of mandoline boxes. But, seldom is its composer named, perhaps because his name, as carefully given above, is hard to pronounce and spell.

This French composer (1844-1926) entered the Paris *Conservatoire* at the age of nine. He composed several operettas and one Grand Opera, *Patrie*, 1886, also several largescale sacred choral works. His one outstanding success was the song *Mandolinata*, composed in 1869 and, like most outstanding popular successes, heard in a number of different arrangements.

Rossini

Some composers need no more introduction today than when they first appeared on musical-box tunesheets well over a hundred years ago, so consistently have their tunes been purveyed by barrel-organs, bands, gramophones, radio and, of course, opera revivals. Rossini is a typical example.

G A Rossini was born in 1792. His father was jailed for welcoming Napoleon's entry to Northern Italy and his mother took him to Bologna where she became a leading lady in opera. Rossini entered the Conservatoire at Bologna as a student of the 'cello and of composition, and specialized in the works of Mozart. By 1816, aged 24, he was director of the San Carlo theatre in Naples and had composed the *Barber of Seville:* he already had a reputation for laziness and when a song was allegedly mislaid he simply wrote on the libretto "Rosina sings an air *ad lib* to suit the occasion". When Donizetti heard that Rossini had composed the entire opera in only thirteen days he said "Why not? He's lazy enough!"—though, of course, he probably said it more picturesquely, and in Italian. Perhaps to counter this reputation, Rossini always claimed that it took necessity to prime his inspiration; and at least one overture was written on the very day the opera opened.

Rossini's 36th and last opera was *William Tell* in 1829. Then he enjoyed forty years of mellow and wealthy retirement. Typically, when asked how well *The Thieving Magpie* (1817) had been received, he replied "I got wearied of bowing".

Other Rossini operas often named on tune sheets are:

Tancredi	1813
An Italian Girl in Algiers	1813

Othello	1816
Cinderella	1817
Semiramide	1823
The Siege of Corinth	1826
Comte Ory	1828

People who have seen the opera *William Tell* are very rare; but so are those who don't know its overture.

I believe it is fairly well known in operatic circles that Rossini composed the aria "Di tanti palpiti" for his opera *Tancredi* whilst cooking himself a tasty dish of rice, which is why they call it the "rice aria." Our musical boxes purvey these operatic gems, and to enable us to compete with such tales I quote an extract from a letter written by Rossini to a friend some time after he had retired from the operatic field in 1829:

'Wait until the evening before the day fixed for the performance. Nothing stimulates one's ardour as much as necessity, the presence of a copyist waiting for your work and the urgings of an impresario who is at his wits' end, tearing out his hair by handfuls. In my time in Italy all impresarios were bald by the age of thirty. I composed the overture to *Othello* in a little room in the Palazzo Barbaja where the baldest and most ferocious of the directors had shut me up by force with nothing except a plateful of macaroni, threatening not to let me out as long as I lived, until I had written the last note. I wrote the overture to the *Gazza Ladra* on the very day of the first performance, under the roof of La Scala, where I had been imprisoned by the director under the guard of four stage carpenters who had orders to throw my manuscript out of the windows, page by page, to the copyists, who were down below waiting to copy it out. If the pages of music failed to arrive, their orders were to throw me out myself. For the *Barber* I managed better: I composed no overture at all. I just took one I had been intending for a semi-serious opera entitled *Elisabetta*. The public was more than satisfied. I composed the overture of *le Comte Ory* while I stood with my feet in the water, fishing, in the company of Signor Augado who was talking about Spanish finance. The overture of *William Tell* was written in much the same circumstances."

Schulhoff

Julius Schulhoff was born in Prague in 1825 and died in Berlin, 1898. He made his local debut as a pianist at the age of fourteen and his first public performance in Paris, helped by Chopin, in 1845. Paris was then the artistic Mecca for pianists. Schulhoff started composing his light but brilliant piano pieces in 1849, and between that year and 1853 made extensive playing tours throughout Europe, including London. His serious compositions included a sonata in F minor, but his tunes most commonly found on musical boxes include the *Grande Valse Brillante*, opus 6; his arrangement of *Le Carnaval de Venise*, opus 22; *Souvenir de Venise*, opus 28; and *Ballade*, opus 41.

Strauss family

The nonchalance of musical box manufacturers about crediting composers on the tune sheets reached a peak with tunes by the Strauss family. No attempt was made to identify the four composers involved; they were all simply listed, if at all, as Strauss.

The following notes will help in sorting them out, though complete sorting is severely hindered because tune sheets often carry colloquial French translations of the original idiomatic German titles, and furthermore the same title was sometimes used by more than one of these four composers. A further complication was caused by some minor composers jumping on to the band-wagon by adopting the pseudonym 'Strauss.'

Strauss I, the father, was born in Vienna in 1804 and became famous both for his compositions and for his orchestra which toured world-wide. He and Joseph Lanner were the first of the Vienna Waltz composers —Lanner leading by a year or two. By 1825 they were already famous and in 1830 Chopin, on a visit to Paris, wrote "Lanner, Strauss and their waltzes dominate everything." They maintained their popularity by a vast output mainly of waltzes and polkas to suit dance-mad Vienna, where tunes were a hit today and forgotten tomorrow. Their life was extremely hectic under the continual strain of composing, rehearsing and conducting, often with encores demanded far into the night. Some of the "magic of the Viennese Waltzes" is said to be due to the second beat of the accompaniment being played a fraction early; whether any musical box tune arrangers achieved this I do not know.

Strauss I married Anna Streim in 1825 and they had six children of whom Johann II, Josef and Eduard were the first, second and sixth. One hears it claimed that they inherited the musical genius of their father. But then, how strange that it appeared in all the sons of Anna Strauss but in none of Strauss's seven children by Emilie Trambusch.

In 1837 Strauss I took his orchestra and his waltzes for the first time to Paris and was greeted with acclaim by a distinguished first night audience which included Adam, Auber, Berlioz, Halévy, Cherubini and Meyerbeer.

In October 1844 his eldest son, Johann Strauss II, had a triumphal first concert in Vienna, his orchestra playing the overture of Auber's *Dumb Girl of Portici*, then some of his own compositions, and finally his father's most popular waltz, *Lorelei-Rhein-Klänge.* This first concert with its great local drama—Strauss I did not want his son to become a musician, and the final waltz was played as a peace-offering—seems to have launched the obviously talented son as THE Strauss. His brother Josef qualified as an architect and engineer but took over the conducting of the Strauss II orchestra in a crisis and with unexpected succcess; he is generally regarded as the most gifted of the three brothers. Young Eduard was an effective conductor but the least talented composer.

Here are the family vital statistics and earliest composing dates which are sometimes a useful clue on the tune sheet—

Name	Born	Died	Started Composing	Highest Opus No.
Johann Strauss I	1804	1849	1820	251
Johann Strauss II	1825	1899	1843	479
Josef Strauss	1827	1870	1853	283
Eduard Strauss	1835	1916	1859	300

Some of their compositions were in collaboration. Some were never given opus numbers. Many were quadrilles and other arrangements from current operas, duly credited in their titles; this causes ambiguities on musical box tune sheets because if, for example, a tune is simply given as *Giroflé Girofla* it could be either an air from Lecocq's opera or a waltz Opus 123 by Eduard Strauss.

In the following lists of a few of their compositions found on musical boxes I have included opus numbers because these give an idea of the tune's date. Tunes by Struass I are rare on lever-wound boxes, and I think I am right in saying that tunes by the other three are extremely rare on keywind. But all four are to be found on discs.

By Johann Strauss I . . .

Philomélen Waltz	op 82
Palm-Zweige Waltz (Branches du Palmier)	op 122
Elektrische-Funken Waltz (L'Etincelle)	op 125

| Lorelei-Rhein-Klänge Waltz | op 154 |
| Radetzky March | op 228 |

By Johann Strauss II . . .

Annen Polka	op 117
Lebenswecker Waltz	op 232
Morgenblätter Waltz	op 279
Juristenball Polka	op 280
Telegramm Waltz	op 318
Leichtes Blut Polka	op 319

Some of his most famous waltzes including *The Blue Danube* (op 314, 1867) and *Tales from the Vienna Woods* (op 325, 1867) are not easily condensed into one minute and are therefore a bit disappointing on musical boxes and, it is worth noting, extremely disappointing to Strauss enthusiasts. I have listed above a few less famous pieces that go well, and in particular the *Lebenswecker* waltz has a stirring second movement, well arranged by Nicole and others on mandolin boxes.

Johann Strauss II also wrote an opera *Ritter Pasman* (1892) and sixteen operettas including . . .

Indigo	1871
Die Fledermaus	1874
The Gipsy Baron	1885
Waldmeister	1895

And in collaboration with Josef he wrote the *Pizzicato Polka* (1869).

By Josef Strauss . . .

Elfen polka	op 74
Wiener Leben Polka	op 219
Sphärenklänge Waltz (Music of the spheres)	op 235
Vélocipède Polka (Bicycle)	op 259
Ohne Sorgen Polka (Care free)	op 271

By Eduard Strauss . . .

Bahn Frei! Polka (Fast Track)	op 45
Doctrinen Waltz	op 79
Liebeszauber Mazurka (Love's charm)	op 84

A complete list (in German) of all the Strauss compositions is available in the Central Music Library, Buckingham Palace Road, London SW1. Favourites are featured every year on New Year's Day in a traditional gala concert in Vienna, usually shown by the BBC with some help from the Johann Strauss Society of Great Britain. Some less well-known items are included among the perennial favourites, the 1981 concert giving the *Waldmeister* overture and *Leichtes Blut.*

Unfortunately the name Strauss on a tune sheet is not certain to belong to a member of the famous family. Sundry minor musicians adopted the name during its first heyday. In particular Isaac Strauss (born Strasbourg 1806, died Paris 1888) composed numerous waltzes and polkas which he sometimes signed 'J Strauss' or simply 'Strauss.' He was a professor at the Paris Conservatoire and he followed Musard as Musical Director of the Court Balls in 1852.

Sir Arthur Sullivan

The main purpose of these notes about composers is to give a general idea of their period and status and to date their works heard on musical boxes. So, in dealing with Sullivan, I face the paradox of ignoring the redoubtable Gilbert, but plenty of excellent biographies are readily available.

Arthur Seymour Sullivan was born in Lambeth in 1842 but soon moved to Camberley when his father became bandmaster at the Royal Military College, Sandhurst. At age 14 he won the Mendelssohn Scholarship at the Royal Academy of Music and this led to him spending three years at the Conservatory in Leipzig. Back in England in 1861, where music composition was at a low ebb, he embarked on a wide range of successful compositions including a collaboration with Tennyson, and he took up a number of teaching and conducting jobs, including the Glasgow Orpheus Choir, Promenade Concerts and the Leeds Festival. He was also the first director of the National Training School, later retitled Royal College of Music.

He first collaborated with W S Gilbert in 1871 and the pair produced 14 operettas in the next 25 years despite periodic rows and Sullivan's spells of chronic ill-health. In 1878 their fourth, *HMS Pinafore,* had a slow start but, after Sullivan played selections from it at the Covent Garden Promenade Concerts, it took off in a big way and during 1879 there were five pirated versions running in New York. Sullivan's earnings for the year 1880 totalled £9988, of which about £6000 came from *Pinafore* and the *Pirates.*

Sullivan was lionized by society and universally liked. He was knighted in 1883. Naturally he felt a bit irked that his fame rested mainly on less serious music; his one grand opera, *Ivanhoe*, was only a semisuccess. Queen Victoria had urged him to compose a grand opera but for a command performance at Windsor Castle in 1891 she chose *The Gondoliers.* His last works were a song in collaboration with Kipling, *The Absent-minded Beggar* (Polyphon Nos. 2627, 10133, 50063) and *The Emerald Isle* which was completed in 1901 by Edward German, hence the two composers shown against the Polyphon series Nos. 10347 to 10351 and 50426 to 50430. He died in 1900 and was honoured with a state funeral in St Paul's Cathedral.

I have listed the Sullivan works most commonly heard on musical boxes in date order. Airs from *Pinafore* seem to turn up most frequently, perhaps due to the tremendous 1879 publicity.

Cox and Box	1867
Onward Christian Soldiers	1872
The Lost Chord	1877
HMS Pinafore	1878
Pirates of Penzance	1879
Patience	1881
Iolanthe	1882
The Mikado	1885
Ruddigore	1887
Yeomen of the Guard	1888
The Gondoliers	1889
Ivanhoe	1891
Haddon Hall	1892
The Grand Duke	1896

Franz von Suppé

Suppé's father was an Austrian civil servant and his mother Viennese. Born in Dalmatia in 1819, he studied law at Padua but turned to music in 1835. After a string of early successes he became Kapellmeister at a Vienna theatre from 1845 till 1862, composing many theatrical scores and becoming friendly with his distant relative, Donizetti. He worked for other theatres till 1882, his compositions including parody versions of Wagner and Meyerbeer operas. He is the earliest Viennese composer whose work is still popular. He was given the Freedom of the City of Vienna in 1881, and died there in 1895.

The best remembered and most popular of his many operettas and musical plays include. . . .

Morning, Noon and Night in Vienna	1844
Poet and Peasant	1846
Pique Dame (Queen of Spades)	1862
Die Schone Galathea	1865
Light Cavalry	1866
Boccaccio	1879
Das Modell	1895

There are many Suppé tunes on disc, including three from *Boccaccio* of which he once said "it was the greatest success of my life." Also, on Polyphon Nos. 1866 and 5625, there is the Coletta Waltz from *Das Modell* which I have not yet seen on a cylinder box tune sheet, though all the others appear from time to time, most commonly the *Light Cavalry* Overture.

Verdi

Giuseppe Verdi, 1813 to 1901, achieved and still achieves the very highest critical acclaim as an opera composer. As a young enthusiast he tried for a scholarship at the Conservatory in Milan but was refused, as lacking musical aptitude. So he persisted with private study and returned to Milan to compose operas in 1837. His first major success and the better-known of his 26 operas are as follows:

Nabucco	1842
Ernani	1844
Joan of Arc	1845
Attila	1846
Macbeth	1847
Luisa Miller	1849
Rigoletto	1851
Il Trovatore	1853
La Traviata	1853
Les Vêpres Siciliennes	1855
A Masked Ball	1859
La Forza del Destino	1862

Don Carlos	1867
Aida	1871
Othello	1887
Falstaff	1893

Such was Verdi's eminence by 1860 that he unwillingly became, at Cavour's insistence, a prestige member of the new Italian Parliament, representing his birthplace, Busseto.

Long before, and typically, a Verdi pupil wrote in an 1846 letter that "Within a few weeks of the first performance of *Joan of Arc* its tunes were heard on the barrel organs of Milan; and after the opening of *Attila* cheering crowds, with torches and a brass band, accompanied Verdi to his lodging."

Musical box arrangers also did well with the Verdi tunes, and for example of the 79 written-up tune sheets illustrated in the Ord-Hume book, 26 have tunes by Verdi and of these 15 are from *Il Trovatore* (The Troubador) or *La Traviata* (The Girl led astray).

The opera *Aida* was commissioned, fee 150,000 francs, for the new Italian Theatre in Cairo. It was a sensational success both there and at its Italian premiere at La Scala, Milan, in 1872. Verdi's popularity and eminence caused people to flock to see and admire this new opera. A young man from Reggio went to Parma to see it and found he was the only one who didn't like it. So he went again but still did not like it, and he wrote to Verdi forecasting that it would soon be banished to the dust of the archives, and requesting the refund of his expenses,—two rail and theatre tickets and two dinners, in all 32 lire. Verdi, in a witty reply, actually forked out 28 lire, disallowing the dinners, on condition that the young man kept away from his operas in the future, to spare him further expense.

In February 1887 Verdi, age 74, turned out what some critics call "the perfect opera," *Othello*. And he rounded off a remarkable life's work with *Falstaff*, 1893, which he claimed he wrote purely for his own pleasure. Tunes from these last two very successful operas are comparatively rare on cylinder musical boxes, due to their late dates. Verdi's span of composing, 1839 to 1893, ran close to the life span of the cylinder musical box.

Weber

A notable fact about the selection of tunes for cylinder musical boxes is that some top class composers whose work included all types of music are represented almost exclusively by airs from their operas. Weber is a good example.

Carl Maria von Weber was born near Lubeck in 1786 into a family with several generations of musical background. Despite a rather nomadic childhood and correspondingly varied teachers, young Weber soon showed his musical talents and by 1800 was giving concerts in Leipzig. His performing and composing gained stature steadily until 1807 when Napoleon defeated the Prussians and in the aftermath Weber was glad to get a job as secretary to the Prussian King's dissolute brother. The machinations of this Duke Ludwig and the moral turpitude of some of the Court circle nearly finished Weber, but he was rescued in 1810 and, after arduous rehabilitation, he got his first key job as *Kapellmeister* of the Prague Opera with full powers to replace the entrenched Italians and to create a new, German Company.

In this he succeeded so well that in 1817 he was appointed *Kapellmeister* at Dresden with the specific task of introducing German romantic Opera to supplant the Italian product. It is generally accepted that Weber did in fact lay the foundations of a German Opera revival and that he acted as a model and an inspiration for Wagner.

Weber's numerous compositions included church music and songs and ballads. Most commonly seen on musical boxes are airs from his ten operas, particularly

Abu Hassan	1811
Der Freischütz	1821
Euryanthe	1823
Oberon	1826

Freischütz means Marksman, and its overture is said to be the first to consist entirely of tunes from the opera. The Oberon overture provides an outstanding example of how appreciation is heightened by knowledge. It starts with a dream-like horn call, and listeners who are unaware of this fail to appreciate the skill of the arrangers in achieving just that effect on a musical box.

Weber died in London in June, 1826, less than two months after his great success at Covent Garden where he conducted the first twelve performances of *Oberon*.

Music Hall Composers

Most of the popular tunes on late cylinder musical boxes came from successful comic operas and musicals; but some were from famous Music Hall hits. One associates them mainly with the later types of coloured tune sheets. Here are three typical and fairly common examples, not now equally well remembered. . . .

Champagne Charlie packed them in at the Canterbury Music Hall, Lambeth, in and after 1865. Music was by Alfred Lee, the song written and performed by George Leybourne, one of whose gimmicks was to drive from one Music Hall to another in a carriage drawn by four white horses.

Tommy make room for your uncle was written and composed by T. S. Lonsdale in 1885 and was made famous by W. B. Flair who sang it with tremendous success over a period of ten years, sometimes at six Halls in one evening.

The Man who broke the Bank at Monte Carlo, music by F. Gilbert, was written and made famous in 1890 by the singer Charles Coburn, real name Colin McCallum. This song (and *Two Lovely Black Eyes*) put him firmly at the top of the bill, and he is also remembered for services to the Music Hall profession, which flourished from 1850 until the 1914 war and then went into decline. I expect this tune kept going for a long time in Pubs on Polyphon 5357.

One hundred years ago, as now, it was not only the merit of a tune that brought fame, but the combination of its launching and timing and performer. Which explains why one often finds apparently unknown, but very attractive tunes on cylinder musical boxes. It also indicates, again, the amount of background interest waiting to be found in tune sheets.

Lyrics

It is extremely rare for a musical box owner to know the words of any operatic aria played by his musical box. Why should he?—being mainly there for the music. Moreover the operas are generally known for their composers, not for their authors or lyric-writers.

Nonetheless the lyric adds a dimension to the music, and knowing it increases one's interest. Furthermore some lyrics express age-old sentiments still commonly expressed today; and as an example, I quote the second of the two verses of an aria ocmmonly heard on musical boxes, "When other lips", from *The Bohemian Girl* by Balfe, 1843, words by Alfred Bunn.

"When coldness or deceit shall slight
The beauty now they prize,
And deem it but a faded light
Which burns within your eyes;
When hollow hearts shall wear a mask
'Twill break your own to see;
In such a moment I but ask
That you'll remember me
  That you'll remember
    You'll remember me."

Music Mystery

A name conspicuously absent from musical box tune sheets is Chopin, 1810-1849. By 1835 he was internationally famous as composer and pianist, he moved in elite musical circles, and his compositions were highly popular. They numbered over one hundred, mainly for piano. Why manufacturers wanting a rousing tune for a drum-and-bells box failed to select Chopin's *Polonaise Militaire*, Op. 40, I simply cannot imagine. Years later its opening bars did international service as the interval signal for Warsaw Radio.

'Ideal' Tunes

There are some tunes which almost everyone would vote ideal for musical boxes, and prominent among them is the *Carnival of Venice*. Nobody knows who originally composed it, but it was first set down by the famous violinist Paganini (1782-1840). He heard it as a popular local air in Venice in the 1790s and he further popularised it and spread it by including it in his repertoire. Both Herz and Schulhoff made popular piano arrangements of it, and it was used as a song in an 1856 opera by Massé, *La Reine Topaze*. Then in 1857 it was used in the overture of an opera by A Thomas entitled, yes, *Le Carnaval de Venise*. So you see it was well liked, and those excellent arrangers of tunes for musical boxes had plenty of ideas to

212

draw on. Perhaps, its most ambitious airing (appropriate term) was by Nicole on Gamme 1818 which was first pinned around 1865 and on which the tune ran for over three minutes.

Music Arrangers

I used to imagine numerous dedicated music arrangers each doing his independent best in getting contemporary popular and operatic music in suitable shape for the cylinder prickers. But, more and more I have gradually come to the conclusion that numerous short cuts wers taken. After all, it is a bit strange to hear almost exactly the same arrangement of *Home Sweet Home* (to take an easy example) on an 1835 Alibert No. 6245 and on Nicole's gamme No. 2615 which was used on serial Nos. 45887 and 8 and 47392 in the 1870-75 period. So one is tempted to conclude that some person or persons gathered together successful arrangements and supplied them, for a fee, to all comers; cheaper and quicker than doing new arrangements from scratch. In a boom year it would make particular sense when there was a shortage of good arrangers. This general plan would be helped by the large degree of standardisation between many makers. It also goes some way towards explaining the narrowly conventional style of so many arrangements; though they vary a lot in their quality they are very consistent in avoiding unconventional effects, such as, for example, bells only passages in a bell box.

Presumably many arrangers worked from home and were available to any maker, which may explain why the boxes made in France by L'Epee have tune arrangements which are indistinguishable in style from the Swiss makers. Perhaps also there was never any getting-together of groups of tune arrangers; if there had been, possibly enough insulting remarks would have been made to sting some of them into being more adventurous. Equally, one can imagine bright ideas being strictly taboo to the conventional makers.

No one seems to know exactly who did the musical arrangements; probably talented musicians who were also competent instrumentalists, but who lacked the special combination of qualities that go to make a notable composer. They certainly succeeded in several tricky jobs—fitting all the tunes to the same abbreviated length, emphasizing the main melody, imitating many orchestral effects, adding those attractive decorating notes known to musicians as ornaments, and at times applying special effects such as forte-piano, mandoline and bells. They also imposed their own interpretations as one can demonstrate by playing the same tune on different boxes; and these interpretations sometimes differed widely in emphasis and style. For example, secondary melodies were sometimes elevated to become the main theme. The decorations or ornaments of the tune are sometimes as attractive as the tune itself, making you want to hear it again, and then again, so that one can well picture an 1870 owner getting "hooked" on a particular tune, as pop fans seem to get hooked today.

But, the big question remains, did the *composers* like these musical box arrangements? The answer to that must be yes. Leading composers like Auber, Rossini, Offenbach and Verdi were all around and flourishing in the 1860s and they must often have heard their tunes and condensed overtures on musical boxes. If they hadn't liked them they would have said so loud and clear. But since they kept quiet, I feel certain they were pleased and even possibly flattered.

10

MUSICAL BOXES IN FILM & FICTION

Early Days

The earliest ode to a musical box is generally agreed to be Leigh Hunt's poem, *On Hearing a little Musical Box.* I think it is also commonly agreed that the poem dates from about 1860, but interestingly that is wrong. It was first published by Leigh Hunt in *The Examiner* on May 19th, 1816. The last of its several reprints was in 1860.

The whole poem of 60 lines is a bit long to give here, but the opening and a few later lines are well worth anybody's space. . . .

> Hallo!—what?—where?— what can it be
> That strikes up so deliciously?
> I never in my life—what? no!
> That little tin-box playing so?
> It really seemed as if a sprite
> Had struck among us, swift and light,
> And come from some minuter star
> To treat us with his pearl guitar.
>
> O thou sweet and sudden pleasure,
> Dropping in the lap of leisure,
> Essence of harmonious joy,
> Epithet-exhausting toy,
> Well may lovely hands and eyes
> Start at thee in sweet-surprise;
> Nor will we consent to see
> In thee mere machinery,

215

But recur to the great springs
Of divine and human things.

Fiction

It is strange how very seldom musical boxes figure in the fiction of their period. They were good descriptive items, one would have thought, giving the novelist plenty of scope for heightening romantic and other scenes.

One of their rare appearances occurs in the excellent 1903 novel by Erskine Childers *The Riddle of the Sands*, when the two Englishmen visit the pilot's house at the entrance to Schlei fiord—just South of Denmark in the Baltic sea:

"After tea we called on the pilot. Patriarchally installed before a roaring stove, in the company of a buxom bustling daughter-in-law and some rosy grandchildren, we found a rotund and rubicund person, who greeted us with a hoarse roar of welcome in German which instantly changed, when he saw us, to the funniest broken English, spoken with intense relish and pride. We explained ourselves and our mission as well as we could through the hospitable interruptions caused by beer and the strains of a huge musical box, which had been set going in honour of our arrival".

According to Jules Verne (assuming accurate translation) early musical snuff boxes lacked an effective on/off control. His short story about a deranged clockmaker, *Master Zacharius*, published in 1874, is set in old Geneva. The house servant, old Scholastique, was always on about the evils of the times. Her talk was non-stop . . . "Nobody tried to stop its course. It was with her as with the musical snuff-boxes which they made at Geneva; once wound up, you must break them before you will prevent their playing all their airs through".

Jules Verne was very up-to-date on phonographs. In *The Tribulations of a Chinaman*, published in 1879, two main characters correspond not by writing but . . .

The envelope bore the Shanghai postmark, but without waiting to examine the outside she tore it open and extracted not an ordinary letter but a sheet of tinfoil marked with some indented dots that revealed nothing until they were submitted to the action of the phonograph, when she knew they would produce the inflexions of his very voice.

216

"A letter!" she cried; "and more than a letter—I shall hear him speak!"

Carefully she laid her treasure upon the surface of a cylinder within; she put the mechanism in motion and distinctly recognized the tones of her lover's voice . . .

It was pretty bad news, but in an early chapter of the novel. Everything came right in the end.

"Saints"

There were about fifty "Saint" novels by Leslie Charteris and numerous films, TV and otherwise, all adding up to a vast quantity of fiction, much of it stranger than truth. Often gangs of international crooks were seeking to acquire goods to which they were not entitled. One such piece of goods was a small musical box, and after numerous thrilling adventures in which the crooks were finally outwitted it was duly acquired by the Saint. But why should the crooks be so desperate to have this modest item? To solve the mystéry was, for the Saint, merely the work of a moment. Quickly removing the cylinder and rolling it on a bit of paper, the resulting pattern of dots revealed a secret formula of international importance.

What an interesting job for the tune arrangers, to combine the formula with an acceptable tune.

Through Different Eyes

The famous Amercan dictionary, Websters, gives musical box as: "*n, chiefly Brit:* MUSIC BOX." And a bit lower down it gives music box as mechanical, mainly clockwork, producer of music. Poets, however, are among those who do not take too much notice of the dictionary, specially when there are problems of rhyme or metre. The simple three syllable word just would not fit so Robert Service took a liberty in *Dan McGrew* . . .

A bunch of the boys were whooping
   it up in the Malamute saloon;
The kid that handles the music-box
   was hitting a jag-time tune . . .

Cinema Fiction

Films of fiction became established in the cinema about the same time as the gramophone became established, and well before the 1920's it was a commonplace device of film directors to portray time lapses and journeys by mixing from shots of rotating gramophone records to shots of vehicles on the move.

What was not commonplace was to see this device used in a period picture whose action took place before the coming of the gramophone, but an interesting example occurs in the Mary Pickford and Leslie Howard film *Secrets*, directed for United Artists in 1932 by Frank Borzage. Here the action to be covered was from the end of a wedding through a train journey to the start of a trek by covered wagon,—all happening in the 1870's. The following shots were used, mixed from one to the next by ordinary lap-dissolves . . .

1. Regina musical box playing, with oval picture in the lid showing train hauled by typical American 4-4-0 locomotive.
2. The train picture filling the screen.
3. The same train in action, approaching the screen.
4. Speeding along railway track.
5. Close view of Regina disc playing.
6. Wagon wheel rolling.

The sound track changed appropriately from "musical box music" to fast train music then ponderous wagon wheel music. The 1870 period of the story was well before disc musical boxes, but who would grumble at a minor anachronism when seeing a nice Regina—even with an unusual picture in its lid.

Steam Organ

Not all fictional references to mechanical music are entirely flattering, as for example the following extracts from a 1947 story by Dornford Yates in which Berry & Co are putting an objectionable neighbour to trial by noise with a steam organ . . .

There is a noise which is made by a gramophone. It may be heard, when the power, which has failed, is restored, if the tune is not yet done and the needle is still on the disc. It is not an agreeable noise. But conceive it magnified beyond all comprehension, and you will have some idea of the introductory movement to *Daisy Bell*. So for some five or six seconds . . . Then the organ was under way, and the well-known melody ranged, like a beast enlarged, the sleeping neighbourhood.

Daisy, Daisy,
  Give me your answer—do . . .

I despair of describing the uproar. Daphne said it was frightening, and she was a mile away. The veil of silence was not so much rent as savaged —when *Hoby's Steam Round-Abouts* laid their simple oblation upon the altar of fun.

Hoby's mouth was close to my ear.
'Good enough, mister?' he blared.
'"The half was not told me,"' I yelled.
'Here he comes', roared Berry, pointing.
A lantern was jerking its way towards us and Withyham arrived, panting.
'Stop this blasted row', he yelled.
'Wot row?' said Hoby.
'This row', howled Withyham. 'This fiendish tune'.
'Change in a minute', said Hobby.
With his words *Daisy Bell* gave way to *The Washington Post*.
'There you are. Wot did I tell you?'
'Stop the machine', screamed Withyham.
'Can't do that', said Hoby. 'Can't disappoint the public'.
'Dam the public', roared Withyham.
'I've people staying with me in that house over there—decent, god-fearing people, and they're half out of their minds'.
'Can't 'elp that', said Hoby. 'I got to open to-morrer at twelve o'clock. An' I got to adjus' the orgin. It ain't no pleasure to me to work all night'.
'*All night?*' screeched Withyham . . .

   Much later, after Withyham signed a document in return for silencing the steam organ, there was a discussion about duress . . .

'A man doesn't make an untrue admission because there's a barrel-organ a fur-long away'.
'Be fair', said Berry. 'Call it a musical box'.
'Be a Jew's 'arp, nex',' said Hoby.

Orchestrions

Most of us, I think I am right in saying, regard Orchestrions as being at the elephantine end of the mechanical music range. They always seem to fill up a complete wall. The smallest I recall reading about is "Lochmann's Original" as described in The Music Box for Summer 1980, Vo. 9 No. 6. This was the Walzen-Orchestrion No. 1 and its size excluding storage stand was about 5 by 3 wide by 2 feet deep. Given dimensions in cms including stand were 235 by 93 by 68. Typical 1905 dictionaries defined them as "a complicated mechanical musical instrument intended to give the effects of an orchestra". The American Webster's dictionary added "somewhat like a barrel organ". The Oxford also has a slightly condescending air, entering it as orchestrina and noting orchestrion as "originally or chiefly USA", and then saying "elaborate kind of barrel-organ meant to give orchestra-like effect".

But orchestrions were certainly not always thought to be necessarily huge, as is proved by the following extract from an 1896 short story by W Carter Platts in which the foolish Mr Tuttlebury has bought a homemade car from a friend and has taken his wife, Maria, for a spin. Of course (then as now) it has gone out of control . . .

"Good Heavens, Maria! The gearing's given way, and we can't stop the blamed thing till all the petroleum's done, and that won't be for forty-five miles!" he gasped in alarm.

"Isn't there a brake?" cried Mrs Tuttlebury.

"Bless you, Maria! You're a woman in ten thousand for resource! There *is* a brake!" and Tuttlebury grabbed hold of a handle, and gave it a desperate wrench, when suddenly there was a preliminary buzz of cog-wheels immediately behind them, and something inside the phaeton began reeling out the tune of "Hurry, little children", like a brass-throated corncrake singing in falsetto.

"What's that?" screamed Mrs Tuttlebury.

"It's an old orchestrion that that confounded idiot of a Wilkinson fixed up under the back seat and geared up to the machinery, and I must ha' got hold of the coupling apparatus instead of the brake. Hullo! Great Scot, we're in for it now, Maria!"

The autocar was now rattling joyously along at the rate of twenty miles an hour; and thirty yards ahead the road merged into another turnpike at a fork. A funeral procession was moving slowly along the other road. The hearse had just cleared the junction when the orchestrion switched off into "Haste to the wedding", with the loud pedal on; and Tuttlebury's autocar swooped down on the procession. The mourning coaches pulled up hastily just in time; but there was no retreat for the

220

hearse. The driver gave one frightened look at the pursuers and lashed up his horses into a gallop. One half of the road was obstructed for half-a-mile, owing to some water pipes being laid down, so that there was no room to pass, and away the hearse flew, doing record time, with the Tuttleburys in hot chase behind it, to the tune of "Keep in de middle ob de road", until the barrel slipped and slid off into "Come where my love lies dreaming", just about the time that the coffin was bounced through the glass side panel and landed in the hedge. What was left of the hearse won that half-mile race by a short length, and pulled up at the side to let the autocar whiz past.

It is sobering to think that in 1896 there were "old orchestrions" for DIY dabblers to build into new autocars.

Elementary

Three small single-tune musical boxes, with movements and cases manufactured by convicts in Dartmoor prison, were featured in the film *Sherlock Holmes and The Secret Code* (USA title *Dressed To Kill*). This was one of the later Rathbone/Bruce films, directed by R.W. Neill for Universal in 1946. Its story was not from Conan Doyle, and it depended on different wrong notes in the same tune on the three musical boxes adding up to a clue which would locate a criminal's loot. Holmes got there first, of course, but one had to admire the Dartmoor tune arrangers.

Background Music

An interchangeable cylinder musical box with bells appears briefly, but plays quite a bit in the film *Holiday* (1938, directed by George Cukor for Columbia). It has a large case on a matching plinth for spare cylinders, but there is no tune sheet. When switched on by K. Hepburn a fairly convincing *click* is heard, but the music is extraordinarily emasculated, suggesting a mere 20-note comb whereas the machine depicted would have at least 70 music teeth. The music completely lacks any bass notes and is without any trills or other decorations, but it plays *The Blue Danube* for about two minutes while some serious dialogue is being spoken by Hepburn and Grant.

So yet again a musical box comes over as *tinkling*. Black mark to Co-

221

lumbia; they could just as well have done it properly . . . or could they? It might have so surprised the audience to hear a good musical box that they would not have listened to the dialogue.

More Absolute Fiction

George Constantine was thirty, a big man, built like a full-back, with a sun-burned, square, almost pugnacious face. He was rounding up some villains called *Scorpio* under a chair-lift in Switzerland when: "Over the clack of the rollers at the supporting pylons he could hear the endless tinkle of cow bells, a sound that always gave him the impression that he was living inside a musical box that for ever played a rather limited tune."

Perhaps no novelist has ever listened to a good cylinder musical box.

APPENDIX
"The New Music" as Advertised in *The Times*, London, 1837-1898.

The first of a long line of musical box advertisements appeared in *The Times* in October 1837:

"LIST of NEW MUSIC, just published, to be had gratis—A quantity of MUSICAL BOXES, playing upwards of 400 airs, overtures, etc, being for SALE, a list of the music is published also the prices of the musical boxes . . . T. COX SAVORY, goldsmith, silversmith, watch-maker. etc, 47, Cornhill."

In those early days the term "musical box" was associated with small movements as in snuff boxes, hence the new wording which appeared in February 1839:

"POWERFUL MUSICAL BOXES, in wood cases, 12 inches long by 5 inches wide, each playing four airs, with the mechanism finished in a very superior manner, are offered for five guineas each. Also a few of the same description, larger sizes, at the following prices:—Six airs £7 7s; eight airs £8 18s 6d; eight airs extra large £14 4s; three overtures £14 14s.—At T. COX SAVORY . . . The small musical boxes, 3½ inches long, continue selling in tin cases price 19s each or in composition shell cases, 25s each . . ."

In July 1839 another advertiser moved in:

"MUSICAL BOXES of superior quality—Messrs KEITH, PROWSE & Co., City Royal Musical Repository, 48 Cheapside, announce to purchasers of real good boxes that they have just received another supply of the best GENEVA BOXES, performing overtures and all the modern English and Foreign melodies. Also the French two-tuned boxes, in painted tin cases 20s; in Composition cases 25s; Musical boxes cleaned and repaired."

The maker was named for the first time by Cox Savory in 1848:

"MUSICAL BOXES. An extensive assortment of fine-toned BOXES, of superior quality, by the celebrated makers Messrs Nicole, Brothers, of Geneva, playing upwards of 600 airs, overtures, etc selected from the works of Mozart, Weber, Rossini, Bellini, Donizetti, etc, together with the most eminent English composers . . ."

A third advertiser appeared in May 1852:

"MUSICAL BOX DEPOT, 54, Cornhill, for the sale of musical boxes made by the celebrated Messrs NICOLE, BROTHERS of Geneva. Small sizes, in composition cases, two tunes, 15s; three, 20s; and four, 40s each. Large sizes, four airs, 14 by 6 by 5 inches £4; six airs, 18 by 6½ by 5 inches £6 6s; eight airs 20 by 6½ by 5 inches £8; and 12 airs, 20½ by 8½ by 7 inches, £12 12s. Containing a selection of all the most popular national and operatic airs, together with hymns etc . . ."

After a month this advertisement was tidied up to read "Messrs Nicole Freres," and in 1853 for a period it added "and other eminent makers." It appeared very regularly for more than a decade.

Business was boosted by the Great Exhibition of 1851 and a fourth advertiser appeared in January 1855:

"MUSICAL BOX REPOSITORY 32 Ludgate Street, St. Paul's—WALES and MCCULLOCH are direct importers of Nicole Freres' celebrated MUSICAL BOXES playing with unrivalled brilliancy of tone the best popular, operatic, and sacred music . . ."

Keith, Prowse were the first to announce, in January 1861, that they had recived another large assortment of boxes, "several of which are of great novelty." But more than a year passed before they actually described these novelties . . .

". . . with flute, bell and drum accompaniments the expressive effects of which upon the ear are exceedingly novel and beautiful."

224

Though it was common to see second-hand pianos advertised in *The Times*, this item in January 1864 was a rarity and perhaps the first ever:

"To be SOLD for £12 10s (cost £21 recently) TWO of NICOLE'S largest MUSICAL BOXES playing respectively eight and 12 tunes of choicest music. They are quite unimpaired by the short time they have been in use, and will be sold either separately or together. May be seen at Wales & Co's, 56 Cheapside."

By the year 1870 *The Times* circulation was over 60,000 often with 16 pages including eight carrying advertisements. For the past ten years there had been as little novelty in musical box advertisments as in those for pianos, which occupied half a column every few days. The stable trio of the decade all appeared regularly:

Keith, Prowse with stock of more than 200 boxes.
Musical Box Depot for Nicole Freres, with new address at 11 & 12, Cornhill, London E.C.
Wales and McCulloch, 56 Cheapside and 12 Ludgate Hill, with largest stock in London of Nicole's genuine musical boxes.

No makers other than Nicole were ever named in these advertisements, but they were named so often that it is a bit surprising that musical boxes were not called Nicoles as, later, cameras were called Kodaks and cleaners Hoovers.

The circulations of several newspapers had overtaken *The Times* by 1870, but it remained the influential, prestige paper so its advertisements continued to be significant though they were a decreasing proportion of total newspaper advertising.

The three consistent advertisers of the 1860s were still active in November 1875—a month which then, as now, signalled the run-up to the Christmas sales drive for luxury goods. Keith, Prowse had expanded their selection of musical boxes to "more than 500 boxes, with all the recent improvements, from £4 to £200," and they urged readers to visit "the new saloons especially devoted to the sale of these enchanting instruments" at 48, Cheapside. The Musical Box Depot at 11 & 12 Cornhill continued to offer "a choice assortment of boxes playing the most popular airs." But it was Wales and McCulloch who came up with the most telling new advertisement, emphasizing their close link with the makers:

"INSTRUMENTS by NICOLE are the perfection of musical mechanism; a delightful resource in the quietude of home or for the entertainment of friends. Superb stock, largest and best in London, with all new and brilliant accompaniments. Prices from £4 to £120, snuffboxes 15s to £3."

By November 1880 both Keith, Prowse and the Cornhill Musical Box Depot had disappeared from *The Times*, but the Wales and McCulloch price range had been extended to £260.

Ownership of Nicole Frères was acquired in 1881 by Charles Brun and he moved the Company headquarters from Geneva to Ely Place, London. The highest serial number made by Nicole before the take-over is No. 47463, and there is no doubt that this was manufactured before 1879, or perhaps earlier, as shown in Fig. 3-19. This could explain why Keith, Prowse advertising stopped in 1879; and it certainly explains the wording, though not the delay, of this October 1885 advertisement:

"SPECIAL OFFER—Musical Boxes—Messrs WALES and McCulloch, 22 and 20 Ludgate Hill, have arranged to SELL, at a large reduction, the whole of their valuable collection of MUSICAL BOXES, by the celebrated Nicole Freres, of Geneva. Catalogues, special issue, gratis and post free . . ."

The same advertisement appeared again several times in October 1886, and on December 11th the first Nicole advertisement appeared, repeated on alternate days till the year end:

"MUSICAL BOXES.—Christmas Gifts.—Messrs NICOLE FRÈRES (established 1815), 21, Ely-place, London and Geneva. Musical boxes, unapproachable in tone, quality, and finish, from £1 1s. Christmas catalogue of newest airs, free."

By November 1887 Wales and McCulloch had widened their wording to "SELLING, at greatly reduced prices, a STOCK of very choice MUSICAL BOXES, by the most eminent makers, . . ." and at the same time Nicole was getting more forceful:

"MUSICAL BOXES—Messrs NICOLE FRÈRES, Geneva (Estab. 1815) Sole London Depot, 21 Ely-place, E.C. Highest Exhibition Awards for quality of tone and finish. Write for No. 76 catalogue gratis and post free. Every description of musical box repaired at moderate charges. Boxes, old, in stock at half price."

A notable new Nicole advertisement appared about twice a week starting in November 1888:

"MUSICAL BOXES, with interchangeable cylinders, by which an endless variety of the most delightful airs can be produced at pleasure.—Messrs. NICOLE FRÈRES invite inspection of the PERFECT INTERCHANGEABLE MUSICAL BOX, of which they are the sole Manufacturers.—21, Ely-place, London, E.C. Geneva, Est 1815. Repairs of every description. Write for Price List No. 5, post free."

That advertisement, with minor changes, appeared throughout November and December in 1889, 1890, and 1891. Then it disappeared,—not surprisingly; numerous patents for disc machines had been published by then and Charles Brun must have realized that the commercial viability of interchangeable cylinders was gone for ever.

Meanwhile Wales and McCulloch continued with rather sporadic advertising till 1896 when they made quite a powerful reappearance with:

"MUSICAL BOXES by renowned makers, who obtained the highest awards at the recent Great Exhibition of Geneva.—New illustrated list of tunes and prices . . ."

They must have enjoyed the lasting prestige as Nicole agents; many Nicole boxes carried their name, incorporated in the tune-sheet design.

After a 2-year gap, Nicole appeared again in December 1895 with emphasis on repair or exchange of boxes: and the same advertisement appeared again in 1896, but with it there also appeared the advertisment which signalled the eclipse of the cylinder musical box era:

"POLYPHON—Music work of the latest construction, is acknowledged by all as the best. It plays by itself many thousand pieces by changing the round metal plates. Purity of sound and durability warranted. Speciality: alarm-watches, £2 15s. German manufacture. Price list free and post paid. Warehouse, ANDREAS HUBER, Jr, Karlsplatz 4, Munchen, Bavaria."

BIBLIOGRAPHY

Chapuis, A. *History of the Musical Box*, trans. Roesch, The Musical Box Society International, 1980.

Clark, John E.T., *Musical Boxes—History & Appreciation*, Allen & Unwin, 1961.

Ord-Hume, A.W.J.G., *Restoring Musical Boxes*, Allen & Unwin, 1979.

Ord-Hume, A.W.J.G., *Musical Box*, Allen & Unwin, 1980.

Tallis, D., *Musical Boxes*, Muller, 1971.

Webb, G., *The Musical Box Handbook, Vol. 1, Cylinder Boxes,* Vestal Press, 1984. Vol. 2, *Disc Boxes*, 1986.

Newcomers to the fascinating field of muscial boxes can quickly extend their knowledge through the Musical Box Societies. These have proved invaluable to everyone interested, with their informative and entertaining meetings and their Journals. . . .

The Music Box published quarterly by The Musical Box Society of Great Britain, 40 Station Approach, Hayes, Bromley, Kent DA15 8DE, U.K.

Technical Journal published three times per year by Musical Box Society International, Box 205, Route 3, Morgantown, IN 46160, U.S.A.

INDEX